"*Ministry Wisdom* is a practical
ministers and those new to leader
fer encouragement for every read
Alvin Lewis and his 'battle-proven' team of writers. I strongly recommend
this book."

Rev. Dr. Charles Myricks, Jr., CODO
National Association of the Church of God

"Imagine a room of friends, each one with a unique journey and a story
to tell. Imagine yourself seated at a table, surrounded by some of the
brightest and best, people you respect and admire. Imagine a moment in
which you can hear from experienced voices pouring into your calling,
making you better at what you do. If you are looking for such a room,
you have found it. In this book. On these pages. An anthology of personal and inspired counsel. Just for you. Just for today. The ministry never
looked better. Walk in and enjoy."

Rev. Jim Lyon, General Director
Church of God Ministries

"*Ministry Wisdom* is a reflection on ministry scope, challenges, and opportunities from highly seasoned church leaders. It will make for a great and
insightful read for young ministry practitioners."

Dr. Owen Facey, Pastor
Genesis Christian Church

"This book addresses a great ministry need of the moment. Our spirituality
has been beset by a socio-cultural divide and insensitivity. Here we have a
powerful addition to our academic kit for ministerial preparation."

Rev. Dr. Amos Farquharson, Senior Pastor
First Baptist Church

"This book is a most useful contribution to pastoral ministry. The many
years of experience combined with the acquired skills and wisdom of the
contributing authors will be of enduring value."

Rev. Dr. Raymond Anglin, Former Pastor
Ascension Peace Presbyterian Church

"The diverse pragmatic issues explored in *Ministry Wisdom* make it a valuable resource for both new and experienced clergy regardless of ministry situation or geography."

Bishop Neville Wilson
Greater Miami Church of God

"This book is a comprehensive reference resource for all pastors. It is timely, is relevant, and addresses many of the challenges faced in ministry today. Highly recommended."

Rev. Karl A. Francis, Lead Pastor
Living Word Open Bible Church

"In the midst of one of the most chaotic and uncertain seasons of our lifetime, *Ministry Wisdom* will empower church leaders and the people they serve to effectively pursue Christ's mission for the church."

Rev. Arthur Conner, Jr., Senior Pastor
Metropolitan Baptist Church

MINISTRY WISDOM

A VALUABLE RESOURCE FOR PASTORS AND MINISTERS

by Alvin Lewis, PhD, MDiv, MS,
and other experienced pastors/ministers

For a free study guide, visit warnerpress.org/ministry-wisdom-download.

Requests for information should be sent to:
Warner Press, Inc.
2902 Enterprise Drive
Anderson, IN 46013

Editor: Kevin Stiffler
Design and layout: Curtis Corzine

ISBN: 9781684343195
Printed in USA

TABLE OF CONTENTS

Introduction: Training beyond the Classroom

American church leaders are troubled by declining seminary enrollments. Some schools have mitigated the loss with extension campuses or online degree programs, yet the overall trend is downward. We live in a time when fewer people are pursuing seminary degrees and fewer denominations require them for ordination.

Does this mean that fewer people are being called to pastoral work? No. We have no shortage of pastoral candidates, but we do have a serious shortage of *qualified* candidates. This is troubling because congregations too often disband due to their ministers being poorly trained.

A poorly trained minister is more likely to preach or teach erroneous doctrine, but that doesn't close churches as often as one might think. A minister's inept handling of a layperson's moral failure is more likely to scatter the flock. If the moral failure is the minister's own, even worse things can happen. Promiscuity, fraud, and scandal can blight the gospel message in a community for generations to come. Like laypersons, pastors may fall into these traps out of ignorance or naiveté, so sound pastoral training is essential for their survival—and the church's.

Ministers gather their knowledge and skills from a wide variety of sources, and it's fair to say that the most deeply held values of a pastor are acquired not in a classroom, but in the experiences of everyday life. The first time a pastor officiates at a wedding, conducts a funeral, or baptizes a new believer, the experience imparts a wealth of practical knowledge. Such memories stay with the pastor throughout the course of ministry. When days of discouragement come, these memories bolster a pastor's commitment to serve. When times of praise come, the same memories remind the pastor that ministry is not a solo endeavor but is always done in partnership with the Lord. And when an unexpected problem arises, the memory of a similar ministry experience may reveal a creative way to cope with the issue.

How does an aspiring pastor get ministry experience? Some colleges require a ministry student to serve a summer internship, complete a preaching practicum, or earn a number of credits in clinical pastoral education, yet these activities do not give a ministry candidate the pastoral skills that can emerge over several seasons of active ministry engagement. An apprenticeship under a seasoned pastor is better suited to that end.

Leaders in the New Testament church used every opportunity to teach upcoming ministers the skills they needed for service. In the centuries that followed, ministry leadership shifted from traveling evangelists to bishops who governed their congregations with a good deal of autonomy. A bishop's preaching and writing became the standard of his congregation's belief and practice. Aspiring priests, called presbyters, attached themselves to his oversight and care.

The growth of cities and the multiplication of churches during the medieval era made it impossible to serve the spiritual needs of an entire city with a single church ruled by a single overseer. Bishops divided their cities into religious neighborhoods (parishes), each served by its own church. This gave rise to several orders of ministry, which permitted a rational division of ecclesiastical labor. But the medieval system was eminently corruptible. This era was notorious for bloodthirsty Crusades, the sale of indulgences, and other infamous church scandals.

The unprecedented prosperity of the Renaissance allowed families to hire their own religious workers for their household staff. This tide of profiteering secularism reached its flood in the sixteenth century, when reformers such as Martin Luther and John Calvin called for a renewed sense of divine call and consecration in their fellow ministers. These firebrands used the new technology of printing to disseminate their ideas to ministry students throughout Europe. They did not need to be physically present to guide their ministry apprentices; their writings accomplished that.

Leading evangelicals such as John Wesley, Charles Spurgeon, and Dwight L. Moody continued this pattern of apprenticeship-by-publication. This led to the establishment of several prominent institutions of higher learning, where these men lectured and their writings became core textbooks. Yet this did not spell the end of "hands on" ministry apprenticeship. Revivals of the late nineteenth century spawned hundreds of city missions where ministry students lived and worked with their mentors.

During this time, evangelists who were identified with the Holiness Revival established city missions that also served as Bible training institutes. These schools extended their sphere of influence by offering correspondence courses for ministers in training. These courses were forerunners of online degree programs offered by many Christian colleges and seminaries today.

Recently, leading African American pastors have established apprenticeship programs to train new pastors. Tony Evans, T. D. Jakes, and Frederick K. C. Price are a few examples. Women ministers such as Cynthia Hale and Cheryl J. Sanders have also established influential ministry apprenticeship programs. Other churches should follow their example. Ministers are less likely to fall prey to moral failure if they are trained under the care of a loving yet not indulgent congregation.

Recent declines in seminary enrollment do not mean that traditional seminary training is obsolete, but a growing number of ministry candidates want to learn the skills of ministry through engagement in a local parish, working alongside a seasoned pastor. They hope to find more ministry accountability and authenticity in a local congregation than in an academic community. They believe a well-designed apprenticeship will bring them into contact not only with a mature pastor who would be a good role model for their ministry, but also with "the community of saints" who will speak candidly into their character formation.

This book was written by ministers of the Church of God (Anderson, Indiana) because ministry apprenticeships have been a significant factor in the growth of the Church of God. The cost of a resident seminary degree is prohibitive for many students, even those with generous scholarship support. This financial obstacle looms large for people who answer a call to ministry in midlife with a family to support. Moreover, pastoral ministry calls for a high degree of spiritual and emotional maturity, which may not be gained through the seminary experience as well as it can through actual engagement in pastoral work.

Written by nearly two dozen pastors, *Ministry Wisdom* conveys the wisdom and skill its authors have gained "in the trenches" of daily pastoral service. Most of the contributors were trained for ministry through apprenticeship to gifted older pastors, so they know the value of sharing this hard-won knowledge with the next generation of pastors. This is not a textbook in the usual sense, but a set of tools designed to deal with the most common challenges of pastoral ministry. You may choose to read it straight through or begin by reading chapters that address specific challenges facing you now. Either way, we believe you will return here again and again to quench your thirst for wisdom in the work of ministry.

Joseph D. Allison
Anderson, Indiana
July 2020

Joe Allison has served as a Christian writer and editor for fifty years. Ordained in 1980 by the Church of God, he has edited Vital Christianity, Pathways to God, and Church of God books and curriculum. Author of eight books, including Hard Times (Warner Press: 2019), he is a member of the Authors Guild, the American Christian Fiction Writers, and the Academy of Religion. Since retiring as editorial director of discipleship resources and curriculum at Warner Press, he continues to serve as a publishing consultant for various Christian authors and publishers.

Acknowledgements

A book of any magnitude requires far more than a single person's skill. Certainly, this statement holds true regarding this work. I am, therefore, appreciative to the many individuals who contributed ideas, concepts, and insights and helped me complete this book.

Special kudos are extended to Joseph Allison for his invaluable counsel and sage advice as I struggled to frame the table of contents. Joe was also helpful to me in conceptualizing a title for the book, *Ministry Wisdom*.

Dr. Edward Foggs, through his wise counsel, provided many suggestions and recommendations that greatly enhanced this book. Edward was extremely valuable in suggesting some of the contributors to this work. Dr. Foggs was also kind enough to write the dedication essay in honor of the late Dr. James Earl Massey.

This book was enriched by the contribution of Curtiss DeYoung in providing the chapter dealing with the preaching wisdom of Dr. Massey. Curtiss, thank you for giving us permission to utilize Dr. Massey-copyrighted materials and for the extraordinary skill with which you were able to compile your chapter.

To all of my writers who dedicated their efforts and made the sacrifice, I am eternally grateful. I want to particularly thank W. G. Robinson-McNeese, James L. Phillips, and Saundra L. McNeese for writing a chapter on COVID-19 with such short notice.

I am also grateful to all the staff and editors of Warner Press for their keen skills in bringing this project to completion. Thanks to Regina Jackson, vice president of product management; Karen Rhodes, editor of adult ministry resources (retired); and Kevin Stiffler, editor of curriculum and church ministry resources.

This book would have been virtually impossible without the support of my three children, Alvin Vaughn, Lydia Janese, and Lystrelle Daneen, who took time off from their jobs and busy schedules to provide loving care to their mother, who is suffering with dementia.

Finally, I extend my loving gratitude to my wife of sixty-two years, Dr. Juanita Lewis, who has labored with me in every aspect of my ministry throughout our Christian union.

Alvin Lewis
Jackson, Mississippi
July 2020

Dedication

This volume, designed to offer wisdom, counsel, and guidance for strengthening and enhancing Christian ministry, is dedicated to the legacy and memory of the late Rev. Dr. James Earl Massey (1930–2018). Dr. Massey, highly esteemed in his own church body—the Church of God (Anderson, Indiana)—was also recognized nationally and internationally. He was a man of many gifts: pastor, stellar preacher, teacher, scholar, professor, dean, counselor, prolific author, lecturer, and consultant. His life influenced generations of clergy, and his influence will extend to generations yet unborn.

I think Dr. Massey would view with appreciation the contents of this book. Each of the writers knew him personally. Much of his ministry was devoted to mentoring persons who were pursuing their call to Christian ministry. These chapters continue the mentoring task to which he devoted his life.

The call to ministry and the challenges of ministry are very demanding. In today's world, they can seem overwhelming. Finding help and encouragement is essential and can be critical to the faithful pursuit of one's assignment. *Ministry Wisdom* endeavors to support that goal.

In this dedication tribute to Dr. Massey, we express our appreciation to him as a trailblazer. He lived at the growing edge of ministry. He opened doors of opportunity for younger and older ministers, both male and female. He modeled ministry at its best. His chief objective, however, was to be an authentic follower of Jesus Christ and a faithful ambassador for the Christian faith.

Were Dr. Massey still with us in bodily presence, I could envision him exhorting us, "Let us not become weary in doing good, for at the proper time we will reap a harvest if we do not give up" (Gal 6:9, NIV). I further think he would recommend the reading of this volume.

Dr. Edward L. Foggs
Anderson, Indiana
July 2020

PART I:

The Nature and Nurture of Pastoral Ministry

1. Preparation for Ministry

by Evelyn Price Wilson

Christian ministry is the activity that happens after we become followers of Jesus and begin to spread our faith. This is in keeping with John 20:21(KJV), where the Lord said, "Peace be unto you: as my Father hath sent me, even so send I you." We may be called to go to another city, state, or country, or just next door. To do ministry is to carry forth Christ's mission into the world. This is the call to every Christian.

In this chapter, I want to focus on the office of the minister, which is where my experience lies. A call to ministry is an awesome responsibility. Oftentimes the call may be one that we prefer not to yield to or obey for various reasons. Some examples of those reasons may be fear, feelings of inadequacy, the desire to earn more money, or simply not being willing to measure up to the commitment of the call.

The Father sent Jesus into a world filled with hatred and jealousy. It was a world in which people's eyes were blind to the truth, because they chose not to see. Hearts were hardened by hatred, envy, and lust. The Father sent Jesus into a world where he would experience loneliness and longing, for he had a mission that no one understood—not even his disciples, the ones to whom he was the closest. He needed friends, companionship, and love because he was human, even though he was God. His mission, purpose, and priority in life were to fulfill that which his Father sent him to do. He was anointed to preach good news to the poor, to proclaim freedom for the prisoners and recovery of sight for the blind, and to release the oppressed. There were many who did not accept him or his message, and many will not accept us today. So are we still called to help pull families out of the murky depths of hopelessness and despair? The answer is yes. Empowered by the Holy Spirit, we enter unchartered territory to proclaim the Word of God.

Some of us may be reluctant to accept our calling because of what we may face. On the other hand, what an honor, what a responsibility, what a challenge it is for Jesus to send us as his Father sent him. Those who accepted Jesus experienced newness of life—abundant life, the kind of life that we would not trade for anything.

Our challenge is to accept the call to ministry and share that hope, joy, and peace with those who don't know Jesus as their Lord and Savior. It is a privilege to be empowered by his words, "As my Father hath sent Me, even so I send you" (John 20:21, KJV). Then he shatters us out of our complacency by his words in John 14:12 (KJV), "Verily, verily, I say unto you, He that believeth on me, the works that I do shall he do also; and greater works than these shall he do; because I go unto my Father." I would like to explore the hopeful side embedded in that declaration, even though failure may occur somewhere along our journey as the Lord perfects us. If we are to accept God's call upon our lives, it necessitates preparation for this awesome ministry. We must preach and minister from experience. In order to do that, we need to have a personal relationship with Christ.

When I was eleven years old, my mother of ten children died. I began to go to church a year before her passing. Some months later, I accepted Jesus as Lord of my life. As I sat in the pews on Sunday mornings, I felt a tugging at my heart to fully commit my life to whatever it was that God wanted me to do. It was all new to me and I did not understand what was going on inside of me. I later began to sing in the youth choir and at the age of fifteen got involved with the youth ministry, as I continued to feel that tugging at my heart. The youth president asked me to be the speaker a few times and I did. I could not shake the feeling that God was calling me to the preaching ministry. Compelled by fear, I made many excuses as to why that could not happen. Those excuses included being too young, not understanding the Bible well enough, having no other preachers in my family, and denying that the tugging I felt in my heart was really the Spirit of God.

Be Sure of Your Calling

An undeniable experience happened to me my junior year of college to resolve the conflict within. I was in the dorm at Warner Pacific College in Portland, Oregon, and my roommate had gone home for the weekend. I was asleep and about 2 AM I heard a voice say, "Evelyn, Evelyn, preach the Word." I sat up instantaneously, with my heart beating faster than usual. I thought my roommate had returned. After that I did not hear anything, so I got up to see who was there. It was just God and me. I went back to my bed, fell on my knees, and wept like a baby. I knew it was God getting my attention. There was no longer any doubt. I was sure of my calling. Spending time praying and studying my Bible took on a new urgency.

During my senior year, I moved back to California and attended Fresno State. I thought all was well, but I later lost my way. I took a class and studied the works of German philosopher Friedrich Nietzsche. One particular concept of his that grabbed my attention was that "God is dead" in the hearts of men and women.

At the same time, I observed and personally experienced the throes of racism. For one year, I developed an intense emotion of hatred in my heart for those inflicting pain on others. I felt miserable and recall the night I sought God in desperation. I asked him to remove that hatred from my heart. He did and replaced it with an unexplainable love that seemed to ignite my heart with fire. I still feel the intensity when I think of the words of Jesus from Matthew 22:37–39 (NIV): " 'Love the Lord your God with all your heart and with all your soul and with all your mind.' This is the first and greatest commandment. And the second is like it: 'Love your neighbor as yourself.' " These commands become more alive each day I practice them.

Immerse Yourself in the Word

Through God's Word, we can draw close to him. To have a ministry that is relevant requires us to have a broad and deep understanding of the Scriptures. During the 1980s while I was living in Kenya, I was hungry for the Word of God. I decided to read three versions of the entire Bible in three years. They included the King James Version, the New International Version, and the American Standard Version. The more I studied, the more I realized I did not know. My initial commitment was to read the Bible in one year, but as my appetite for understanding increased I continued on this journey for the next two years.

As I read, I better understood what God's plans were for my life: " 'For I know the plans I have for you,' declares the LORD, 'plans to prosper you and not to harm you, plans to give you hope and a future' " (Jer 29:11, NIV). Reading the Bible filled my heart with joy: "When your words came, I ate them; they were my joy and my heart's delight, for I bear your name, LORD God Almighty" (Jer 15:16, NIV). Studying God's Word equipped me for battle: "Therefore put on the full armor of God, so that when the day of evil comes, you may be able to stand your ground, and after you have done everything, to stand…. Take the helmet of salvation and the sword of the Spirit, which is the word of God" (Eph 6:13, 17, NIV). Declaring God's Word increased my faith: "Faith comes from hearing the message, and the message is heard through the word about Christ" (Rom 10:17, NIV). I learned that studying and obeying God's Word would bring me delight and prosperity: "Blessed is the one who does not walk in step with the wicked or stand in the way that sinners take or sit in the company of mockers, but whose delight is in the law of the LORD, and who meditates on his law day and night…. Whatever they do prospers" (Ps 1:1–3, NIV).

Fast and Pray

Fasting is defined as voluntarily going without food in order to focus on prayer and fellowship with God. There are different types of fasting; I will share three of them.

The regular fast is done by abstaining from solid food. One example is Jesus' fasting for forty days in the wilderness: "For forty days he was tempted.... He ate nothing during those days, and at the end of them he was hungry" (Luke 4:2, NIV).

A second type of fast is called the partial fast. This diet consists of refraining from certain kinds of foods: "At that time I, Daniel, mourned for three weeks. I ate no choice food; no meat or wine touched my lips; and I used no lotions at all until the three weeks were over" (Dan 10:2–3, NIV).

The third kind of fast is called the full fast in which there is no food and no drink: "For three days [Saul] was blind, and did not eat or drink anything" (Acts 9:9).

I know some Christians think fasting, coupled with prayer, is outdated. But it is a Bible-based discipline, appropriate and relevant in the church. If you have ever been in a situation where you needed a breakthrough, and you knew only God could help, you understand what I mean.

While serving as dean and an educator at Kima Theological College in Kenya, I learned how to fast and pray. I met in one of the classrooms with thirteen students at 6 AM each day for a month, to pray and seek God's guidance and provision. The first two weeks, I went on a regular fast with just water, which was a challenge for me. Prior to that, I had not gone longer than three days. My students began to enquire about my health, as I walked slower and felt weaker. They were not aware of my fast, and I was not led to share that information with them. Though I was weak, during the nights I slept like a baby and later my strength began to return.

Initially, the reason I asked the students to meet for prayer was because they were feeling distressed. Some needed extra money in order to stay in school. Others were concerned about sickness among family members at home. Seven of the students were from Nigeria and could not easily go home for emergencies. They needed spiritual breakthroughs. After three days, we got our first praise report. God answered a financial request. As we continued to gather and pray each morning while it was still dark, we received reports of God's blessings. Two children who had malaria got well, one wife's love for her husband was restored, and another student received a paid internship while continuing his studies. One student prayed for rain so he would have crops, and God answered those prayers.

The classroom could not contain the praises of that group of students! Some ran outside shouting and glorifying God. Others fell on their knees, not able to hold back their tears of joy. I felt God's anointing on me as I re-dedicated my life to him. I felt a holy boldness like never before when I preached and taught his Word. Out of that nucleus of thirteen, we now have dedicated pastors in Kenya, Nigeria, and the United States.

Develop Godly Character

Our character starts in the heart, a place where God alone can see. The psalmist wrote in Psalm 139:23–24 (KJV), "Search me, O God, and know my heart: try me, and know my thoughts: And see if there be any wicked way in me, and lead me in the way everlasting."

God sees our hearts and knows our intentions. Even while we are preaching the message verbally, we should see *ourselves* as the message. Be aware that people see you before they see or hear what you do or say. To have an effective ministry, we need to have godly hearts.

Commit to Quiet Time with the Father

The most precious time of the day is the quiet time we spend with God. Jesus gave us examples of this experience when he retreated to secluded places to commune with the Father. Mark 1:35 (NIV) says, "Very early in the morning, while it was still dark, Jesus got up, left the house and went off to a solitary place, where he prayed." Luke 5:16 (NIV) says, "Jesus often withdrew to lonely places and prayed."

We nourish our bodies with physical food; our souls need nourishment as well. We receive that nourishment during quiet times when we prepare our hearts to hear from God. As we focus on the Father, we eliminate distractions Satan places in our way in an attempt to rob us of a blessing. Our goal is to follow Jesus' example by praying for others as well as for ourselves. This should be a time of thanksgiving and focusing on the Word.

Maintain Your Health

Our bodies are temples of God, and we need to take care of them. Paul instructed in 1 Corinthians 6:19–20 (NIV), "Do you not know that your bodies are temples of the Holy Spirit, who is in you, whom you have received from God? You are not your own; you were bought at a price. Therefore honor God with your bodies." Too many of us take our health for granted. God values our bodies and so should we. Good health helps to prepare us for what the Father called us to do.

I am reminded of a conversation I had with my daughter Adrienne Wilson, who is a physician. She shared that we are just as much our physical selves as we are our spiritual, mental, and emotional selves; all are important. If the physical contains the spiritual, should not the temple be suitable to house God within? We cannot fill ourselves with spiritual food in church, then ignore the physical and sit down to "poison" on the dinner plate. To be whole, we must be spiritually and physically fit. An abundant life is our birthright and can only be experienced through a healthy vessel: "The thief comes only to steal and kill and destroy; I have come that they may have life, and have it to the full" (John 10:10, NIV).

Some things we can do to keep our temples healthy include eating nutritiously, getting adequate sleep, being physically active, and taking regular vacations. If you are married, schedule regular times for a date night. Investing in your marriage will pay significant dividends.

Get a Good Education

Ministers, of all people, should be educated. The Scriptures are full of instructions to live lives full of learning, wisdom, and knowledge: "The LORD gives wisdom: from his mouth come knowledge and understanding" (Prov 2:6, NIV). As a teacher, I studied to obtain a certificate to teach in public schools. As a stockbroker, I studied to obtain a license to manage the financial portfolios of my clients. As a minister, I studied to get a ministerial license and a degree in Christian education to teach and to preach.

Knowledge is important, but we also need wisdom. As ministers, it helps us to apply our knowledge and equips us with discernment. Circumstances arise when we need discernment to know what to do, what to say, and how to read people and situations. "Get wisdom, get understanding; do not forget my words or turn away from them. Do not forsake wisdom, and she will protect you; love her, and she will watch over you. The beginning of wisdom is this: Get wisdom. Though it cost all you have, get understanding. Cherish her, and she will exalt you; embrace her, and she will honor you" (Prov 4:5–8, NIV).

Be Flexible

It is good to have plans and be purposeful and intentional. However, circumstances may change and require us to be flexible. We need to remember our main goal is to serve Christ and his people. Paul said in 1 Corinthians 9:22 (NIV), "To the weak I became weak, to win the weak. I have become all things to all people so that by all possible means I might save some."

After living in Kenya for a few months, I was asked to speak at a women's convention in Western Province. Everything was going great; I poured my heart out to the audience, and the altar was full. After praying and working with the women, everyone went back to their seats, and I also sat down. It had only been about two minutes and I was still trying to get my breath back when the chairwoman of the convention asked me in Luhya to please preach another sermon. When my interpreter told me what she said, I thought she was joking. I just smiled and sat there, thinking I did not clearly understand, but then she repeated the request. It was the first time for me to preach two sermons in a row and the second one without notes. I got up, took a deep breath, grabbed some holy boldness, quoted a Bible verse, and started speaking. I began to say things I was not aware I knew. As the Spirit helped me, I started walking up and down the aisles where the women sat. I had become very emotional. They were amazed as well as I. When I finished, all the women got up and started walking toward the front of the church. The women's leader prayed and praised God. We had a glorious time. That day I learned how to be flexible.

Have Mentors and Those to Hold You Accountable

Mentors are an important tool available to us in ministry. They teach and guide us based on their own experiences. My mentor focused on character and personal growth. There were times she offered simple truths that challenged my self-esteem. I swallowed my pride, followed her advice, and witnessed the growth that took place within me. She also held me accountable for the disciplines I want to continually cultivate in my life.

Conclusion

As you prepare for Christian ministry, seek to confirm your calling. Dig deep into God's Word. Fast and pray. Strive for godly character. Spend time alone with the Father. Focus on your total self. Be a lifelong student. Be flexible. Have a mentor and be accountable. Accept the call God has placed on you and share that hope, joy, and peace with those who don't know Jesus as their Lord and Savior.

Recommended Books

Battlefield of the Mind: Winning the Battle in Your Mind by Joyce Meyer

Made for Paradise: God's Original Plan for Healthy Eating, Physical Activity, and Rest by Patricia Hart Terry

Views from the Mountain: Select Writings of James Earl Massey

When Thou Prayest by James Earl Massey

About the Author

Evelyn Price Wilson is the mother of three sons and two daughters. She lives in Chandler, Arizona, where she has fostered teenage boys for the past fifteen years. She is a graduate of California State University, Fresno, and the Anderson University School of Theology.

Evelyn spent several years as a schoolteacher and administrator, and she and her husband pastored churches in Arizona and Indiana.

Evelyn and her family were commissioned as Church of God missionaries to Kenya from 1981 to 1990. While in Africa, she held various positions as a pastoral trainer, as dean of Kima Theological College, and with Women of the Church of God. After returning to the United States, Evelyn served with the Board of Christian Education of the Church of God. She studied and obtained a stockbroker's license, also working again in the public schools.

Now retired, Evelyn continues to foster teenage boys. She enjoys traveling, and she stays involved in ministry by officiating weddings and accepting speaking engagements. One of her greatest joys is spending time with her grandchildren.

2. What Am I Getting Into?

by Alice J. Dise

A minister can be defined as a servant; one who serves the church as pastor, assistant, associate, or leader of a special ministry (e.g., youth, Christian education, music, etc.) on a full-time or part-time basis. Despite the many directions or courses of action that the call to ministry can take in a person's life, it is clear that ministry is about serving. Whether in the pulpit as a prophet or priest, in the pews, or beyond the walls of the sanctuary, a minister is called to serve. Ever since Jesus called a group of followers to "fish for people" (Matt 4:19, NIV), thousands of men and women have answered the call to serve and become ministers of the gospel of Jesus Christ. The ministry gifts are varied, but the primary focus of all Christian ministry is salvation and bringing men, women, boys, and girls to the knowledge and acceptance of Jesus Christ as Savior.

Each person called into ministry is uniquely gifted and talented to fulfill God's call in his or her own way. Age is not a factor. Some are called at a very young age, while others are much older and heed the call after many years of church attendance.

Affirming Your Call

In Luke 4:18 (NIV), Jesus affirmed his call to ministry: "The Spirit of the Lord is on me, because he has anointed me to proclaim good news to the poor. He has sent me to proclaim freedom for the prisoners and recovery of sight for the blind, to set the oppressed free." It is good for new ministers to use this as a template for affirming their own call to ministry. Is it your conviction that God has anointed you to proclaim good news to the poor? Has he instructed you to proclaim freedom for those who are bound? Has he asked you to proclaim recovery of sight for the physically and spiritually blind? Has he called you to set the oppressed free? If you can answer yes to these things, then affirm in your heart that God is calling you to ministry.

The Source, the Service, and the Specialty

Once you have felt an inner compulsion to serve and then affirmed God's call, you might ask, "Where do I go from here?" New ministers (and even seasoned ones) must remember three things:

- *God is the source of your call.* The Bible says in 1 Samuel 3:8–10 that Samuel heard a voice calling his name. It wasn't until he had heard the call three times and Eli the priest confirmed it was God's voice that Samuel was convinced God was calling him.

- *The call to ministry is a call to service.* Jesus said, "Whoever wants to become great among you must be your servant.... For even the Son of Man did not come to be served, but to serve, and to give his life as a ransom for many" (Mark 10:43, 45, NIV). True servants give of themselves, are accountable to an owner or employer, and have a job or responsibility.

- *God calls ministers to* specialized *service.* It is God who determines the area of ministry in which you serve based on the talents and gifts he has provided to you. Do not be limited by what you think you can or cannot do; rather, be open to study and learn.

Be Committed!

Calling is what God does. Commitment is what people do in response to God's call in order to fulfill the obligations of ministry.

Commitment requires acceptance. The first challenge of ministry is acceptance by saying yes to God's call. Do not think it strange if you have to struggle with the decision to become a minister. Contrary to what many believe, people do not readily choose to become ministers. The decision to commit to God's call often takes many long hours alone with God in prayer in a private Gethsemane before coming to the decision to commit to service.

Commitment requires acknowledgment. The sooner you acknowledge your call, the sooner you will be on your way to discovering God's plan for your ministry. Tell your spouse, your family, and your friends about your decision. Speak with another minister, perhaps someone who has followed a similar path in ministry that you've chosen. Consult with your pastor. Don't be put off by those with negative or pessimistic views. People may not believe you immediately, but if you are true and faithful to your calling, they will become convinced over time.

Commitment requires counting the cost. Prayerfully take an appraisal of what the call to ministry will require of you. Ministry is hard work. It is characterized by one's faith and confidence in God, steadfastness and unwavering pursuit of purpose, and hard work that requires action and a dedicated effort. Jesus said,

"Suppose one of you wants to build a tower. Won't you first sit down and estimate the cost to see if you have enough money to complete it?" (Luke 14:28, NIV).

Commitment requires preparation of the inner self. In Ephesians 3:16–19 (NIV), Paul gave an important revelation about the effects of preparing one's inner self: "I pray that out of his glorious riches he may strengthen you with power through his Spirit in your inner being, so that Christ may dwell in your hearts through faith. And I pray that you, being rooted and established in love, may have power, together with all the Lord's holy people, to grasp how wide and long and high and deep is the love of Christ, and to know this love that surpasses knowledge—that you may be filled to the measure of all the fullness of God."

Commitment requires discipline. The first lesson a minister needs to learn is discipline. Having a disciplined prayer life and enough discipline to systematically read, study, and meditate on God's Word takes purpose, effort, and time. The minister's purpose is to serve effectively by reaching people for Christ and convincing them of his saving grace. Because there are so many distractions in ministry, a deliberate effort is necessary to bring the mind and the spirit together as one under the subjection of God's will through prayer. And being committed to sharing God's Word requires the minister to first spend time communicating with him. How much time should be spent in prayer? Obviously there is no set limit, but those who approach prayer in a hurry are in effect saying they don't have time to talk to or listen to God. Remember, communication is a two-way channel; we keep ourselves open so we can hear from God more clearly.

Commitment requires study. Ministry is a profession as well as a calling. Commitment to ministry, therefore, requires that one prepares to "rightly divide the word of truth" (2 Tim 2:15, KJV). The minister must study God's Word for illumination and direction. The Bible is the main source of information. Other historical or philosophical texts may be used for life application, but they must line up with the Bible.

Commitment requires action. Ministry requires work, and work implies action. This means that in ministry, as in life, you do what you do in obedience to God, the one who gives you the action plan: "See to it that you complete the ministry you have received in the Lord" (Col 4:17, NIV).

Understanding the Segments of the Worship Service

As a minister, you will be involved specifically in one or more parts of the worship service. The order of service is not the same in all churches, but here are some possible segments:

1. *Call to Worship.* This is an appeal to congregants to enter in and worship, calling the church "to order." The call may take the form of a prayer, a reading from the Scriptures, or a simple summons. It is the first order of business conducted in the worship service. A greeting or brief comments relative to the worship experience may be given.

2. *Invocation.* The invocation is a prayer that honors God and invites his presence into the worship service. The prayer need not be long; it can be given by the minister or it can be read directly from the Bible. In some churches, the Call to Worship and the Invocation are the same.

3. *General Prayer.* Sometimes referred to as the Pastoral Prayer, this prayer lifts the concerns of the church. The person who is asked to perform this prayer ought to be attuned to the needs of the congregation. As you plan to offer this prayer, let the Holy Spirit guide your words.

4. *Reading of Scripture.* All services should include the reading of God's Word. The reading may be done responsively (with audience participation) or by one reader. Whenever possible, the scripture selection should relate to the overall theme of the service.

5. *Sacred Music.* This music can include the choir, the congregation, soloists, groups, or instruments. A variety of song types should be selected, including songs of praise, affirmation, salvation, and hope.

6. *Church Announcements.* Attention should be given to preparing and presenting the announcements so that members will be made aware of the church's events and happenings, which are opportunities and requests for service. Verbal announcements are significant because people tend to pay attention to and remember what they hear as well as what they read.

7. *Welcoming of Visitors.* There should always be an acknowledgment and welcome given to visitors to join the congregation in worship.

8. *Tithes and Offerings.* The giving of tithes and offerings is biblically based. Such giving represents obedience and thanksgiving to God.

9. *Offertory Prayer.* This is a prayer of thanksgiving and dedication of tithes and offerings. It does not need to be long.

10. *Meditation.* This is an opportunity to listen to and hear from God. It is a time for reflection and contemplation.

11. *Sermon Prelude Prayer.* The minister acknowledges the need for God's anointing prior to the beginning of the message. Often the pastor will offer this prayer himself or herself, but other times someone else may be asked to do so.

12. *Sermon.* The proclamation of God's Word is the apex of the worship service.

13. *Invitation to Discipleship.* The invitation to accept Christ or join the church offers an opportunity for individuals to reflect on and respond to the total worship experience. It may be followed by conviction, contrition, acceptance of Jesus Christ, and even personal praise and thanksgiving.

14. *Altar Prayer.* The time of Altar Prayer is designed to lift up any special needs or concerns of the church before the Lord. It may be led by the pastor or someone else he or she has designated.

Altar Methodology

A minister will be called on to serve at the altar. The altar worker assists people with encouragement and prayer to respond to what has already taken place. Comments and prayers are most helpful when they relate to the sermon and enforce its theme.

Altar workers should be compassionate, trustworthy, and have a good knowledge of God's Word. They should have a concern for lost souls, know how to intercede for others in prayer, be able to communicate, be sensitive to the leading of the Holy Spirit, and have a desire for the salvation of souls. They should be conscious of personal hygiene (breath and body). Altar workers should not divulge secrets shared by the seeker, and they should not give counsel at the altar except when leading someone to Christ.

Altar methodologies vary from church to church depending on a number of factors, including culture, denomination, and tradition. The following suggested methodology will provide guidelines for churches that follow a formal altar call, allowing seekers to come forward for prayer:

- *Be welcoming.* Approach those who come forward with a smile and a friendly gesture.

- *Body contact.* If the seeker is kneeling, kneel beside him or her if possible. If this person is already praying, the altar worker should also pray silently momentarily before interrupting. Grasping the seeker's hand in a gentle way may be appropriate, or perhaps putting an arm around the person's shoulder. Avoid an embrace unless you know it is okay (especially with members of the opposite sex).

- *Introduce yourself as an altar worker.* Perhaps say something such as, "My name is _____. Would you like me to pray with you? How may I pray with you? How may I help? Is there something special that you'd like me to pray about?"

- *Preparing to pray.* Listen attentively to what the seeker is saying. Is the person seeking salvation? Is this a reaffirmation of faith? Are there special needs or burdens? Be sure you understand the need, then indicate what you will be praying for, summarizing or articulating the need.

- *Praying with or for the seeker.* Address the needs that are at hand. Pray softly. The prayer is between you, the person for whom you are praying, and God.

- *Wrapping it up.* Do not pressure someone to make a commitment. If a commitment to Christ is made, this should be expressed publicly to be celebrated by the congregation. Remain with the person until this has been done. If the person is shy or unwilling to speak publicly, you may speak for her or him, giving the content of the seeker's testimony. Introduce the person by giving her or his name and the facts of this person's commitment. The minister can introduce the seeker to the church and give further directions. If no commitment is made, allow the person to return to her or his seat quietly. Assure this person of your continued interest and prayers for the problem or concern that was shared with you.

The following Bible passages can be useful for those working at the altar.

FAITH PASSAGES
- Psalm 37:5
- Psalm 56:3
- Matthew 21:22
- 2 Corinthians 5:7

PRAYER PASSAGES
- Philippians 4:6
- Hebrews 4:16
- 1 John 5:14

THE PLAN OF SALVATION FROM ROMANS
- Romans 3:23 (the reality of sin)
- Romans 3:10 (none are righteous)
- Romans 5:12 (sin and death through Adam)
- Romans 5:6, 8 (Christ died for us)
- Romans 6:23 (the penalty of sin)
- Romans 10:13 (call on the Lord to be saved)
- Romans 10:9–10 (confess Christ and believe)

- Psalm 51:5 (we are born in sin)
- John 3:16 (the gift of salvation)
- John 5:24; 6:44–47 (assurance of eternal life)

Visiting the Sick

All ministers visit the sick or shut-ins in the hospital, nursing homes, or private homes at some point. The following guidelines are intended especially for ministers in training. However, there are exceptions to all rules. When in doubt, pray for God's guidance or consult with a more experienced minister. Pray beforehand in order to prepare yourself spiritually and mentally to make a visit.

At a hospital, be aware of administrative requirements, visiting hours, and procedures. Pay attention to "isolation" or "no visiting" signs and respect them. Wear gloves or a mask when suggested by hospital or family, and cleanse your hands with soap and water or hand sanitizer before and after leaving the bedside. Avoid using the patient's private washroom. If the door is closed, make sure it is okay to enter the patient's room. Try to have some knowledge of the patient's condition before you visit and find out if the visit is acceptable or desired. Excuse yourself when the doctor comes in unless he or she asks or permits you to stay. Pay attention to mechanical apparatus, and be careful of where you sit or stand; sitting on the patient's bed may cause discomfort. Excuse yourself when the patient's meal is being served, unless you are asked to stay or it is necessary for you to help the patient eat. If you find other visitors or family members present, excuse yourself unless you are asked to remain.

For any visit, beware of your body language; pity, fear, judgment, and love are all expressed through your actions and demeanor. Be a good listener. The patient or family member(s) may need to talk about their concerns and fears; do not downplay the reality of their physical or mental pain. Complete your visit in a timely manner. Offer to pray with the patient (or family), read from the Scriptures, and then leave. Keep all conversations confidential; it is not your place to discuss the condition of someone you are ministering to, even if it is with the patient's family. Don't give unsolicited advice regarding treatment. Don't be a prophet of doom; sick people don't need to be reminded of the seriousness of their illness, nor do they need to be compared to another person with the same type of illness. Limit your personal opinions and stories to ones of encouragement. Don't make promises of healing unless you are certain of God's will. Encourage the patient to have faith in God, and let this person know that you also have faith in God for her or his healing.

Leading Someone to Christ

Every minister of Jesus Christ wants to hear someone ask, "What must I do to be saved?" It is good to memorize as much of the following information as possible, or carry a copy of it with you to enable you to answer questions about salvation clearly and succinctly.

What must I do to be saved? Believe on the Lord Jesus Christ (Acts 16:31). Believe that God loves you and wants to save you. Believe that Jesus died to save you and that he has paid the price for your sins.

When can I be saved? "Now is the time of God's favor, now is the day of salvation" (2 Cor 6:2, NIV).

How can I be saved? By accepting Jesus as Savior and Lord. Accept him by faith (John 20:29). Accept him as Savior; he died for your sins (Matt 20:28). Accept him as Lord; he is the one you will love, worship, and obey (Luke 6:46). Repent of your sins (Rom 3:23). Commit to turn away from sin. Pray, asking to be forgiven by God. Ask God to save you. Thank God for forgiving and saving you. Acknowledge Jesus as Lord and Savior (Rom 10:9).

Here is a sample prayer someone can repeat after you: "Dear God, thank you for sending Jesus to die for me on the cross that I might be saved. Please forgive me for all my sins and save me; cleanse my heart. I accept you as my Lord and Savior. Thank you. Amen." The person who has been saved should be encouraged to tell family and friends of this decision.

The minster should pray for the enabling power of the Holy Spirit to lead a person to Christ. Believe that God wants to save the seeker. Speak to the core of God's plan for salvation, explaining each point as you move along. An opportunity to teach about how to live a Christian life will come later. The minister should tell the seeker that we can know we are saved because God has said it.

Conclusion

If you feel that God is calling you to ministry, affirm that call! Look to God as your source of strength as you prepare to serve others and identify an area or areas of specialized service, and be committed to the preparation and discipline necessary for fulfilling your call. Understand how you will be involved in the worship service, at the altars, or visiting the sick, and be ready to help lead someone to Christ if the opportunity arises. You are embarking on an incredible journey full of blessings as you follow the Lord's call.

Recommended Books

The New Manners & Customs of Bible Times by Ralph Gower

Responding to the Call of Ministry: A Study Manual and Workbook for Ministers by Alice J. Dise

The Star Book for Ministers by Edward T Hiscox

Unger's Bible Dictionary by Merrill F. Unger

The Worshiping Church: A Guide to the Experience of Worship by James Earl Massey

About the Author

Rev. Alice J. Dise is the body life pastor emeritus of Vernon Park Church of God in Chicago, Illinois. She was ordained as a minister in the Church of God in 1989. During her more than forty years of service, Dise trained new ministers, chaired the ministerial staff, and was superintendent of the Sunday school. In addition to her church responsibilities, she was featured as keynote speaker or teacher at many local and national Christian events.

After receiving a bachelor's degree in Christian Studies from Trinity College in 1985, Rev. Dise became the editorial director for vacation Bible school curriculum at Urban Ministries, Inc. Her contributions to the field of Christian education have been widely recognized. Rev. Dise is the author of *Responding to the Call of Ministry: A Study Manual and Workbook for Ministers* and a contributor to *Journey to the Well* and has also written numerous magazine articles.

3. Healthy Pastors and Healthy Churches

by James Sparks

The church is a living organism and, as such, should be healthy and growing. We sometimes fall into the mistaken belief that if we aren't baptizing people by the hundreds then our congregation is not growing. Not all congregations—indeed, not all Christians—are always in the same place as others. There are stages of growth. None of these stages happen overnight, and they often require an agonizing amount of sweat, money, time, and patience.

Proper Focus

Any institution eventually makes its own survival first priority, which usually means a preservation of the status quo. The majority of time and money goes into preservation: building maintenance, building improvements, program management, and staff. We all acknowledge that those issues must be addressed. The difficulty is when these things become the primary focus of our endeavors and our dollars. One must honestly ask how much is being spent to fund missionaries, assist the homeless, prevent exploitation, and address other ills of society. How much time is being spent on church workdays and potluck dinners compared to that spent mentoring teenage mothers, prison parolees, and victims of abuse, addiction, and violence?

Far too many congregations seek volunteers to serve as ushers, greeters, tellers, worship leaders, instrumentalists, and teachers—in other words, to keep the institution operating—and then wonder why no one has the time or energy to spend with the hurting in the neighborhood. Far too many congregations view visitors to their facility as adversaries—people who will eventually cause them to change the way they have always done things—or as potential workers in their institution. Far too many congregations operate in a manner similar to the local Rotary Club or Elks Lodge: existing for their own pleasure. Far too many congregations blend into their communities much like the local library: a beautiful structure where people come and go but never in large numbers. Far too many congregations are busy doing "church work" but seem to have forgotten "the work of the church." If our commission is to "go" (Matt 28:18–20), then we must honestly ask why we spend so much time and money in and on a single facility.

Many have left the modern church because they were seeking to be touched spiritually and valued honestly but finally grew weary of being fodder for the machinations of a club. I believe they will be drawn to the One who is high and lifted up, but not to another organization that consumes their time and drains their energy. Somewhere along the line, we've become so institutionalized that the passion of Jesus no longer burns in our hearts. This is about more than a fall and spring revival where we remind ourselves to be holy; it is about a "social holiness," where we become the hands and feet of Jesus to those in our communities.

Core Values

The pastor and leadership of any congregation should be able to identify and voice the congregation's core values. These are the elements that are important to a congregation and its identity.

I was once invited to serve as a consultant to a congregation that was declining in numbers. Before I met with the leaders, I asked to view key congregational documents: by-laws, annual reports, budgets, and expenditures. The budget for the previous five years had steadily increased facility maintenance from $15,000 to $25,000, but the outreach budget had remained steady at $200 annually. When I arrived at the church for the meeting, I saw a gorgeous facility located on a corner lot on the outskirts of the community. Inside, everything was sparkling clean, well-lighted, and carefully tended. During the meeting I learned that the outreach budget was spent by donating $200 every Christmas to the community food bank.

Other churches pride themselves on singing from the hymnal, while still others boast about never singing from the hymnal. They may not put it in that terminology, but careful observation of worship experiences can reveal a great deal about a congregation's core values.

Additional examples can be given. The key, however, is to have the congregation—or at least the congregational leadership—understand the nature of the core values, and whether they can be used positively or need to be changed when they are negative.

Prayer

As pastors, our strongest and most effective weapon is prayer. Prayer possesses both the caliber and range needed in our battle with Satan. Prayer can reach beyond the range of our vision with a power far greater than we can imagine. The real miracle of prayer is not that God answers our prayers; it is that God hears our prayers. The greater miracle is that our prayers for lost souls are already on the heart of God and he is eager to hear and answer.

Regrettably, we have created a poor example of the transforming power of prayer for our people when our prayers spend so much time focused on physical needs rather than spiritual needs. In smaller congregations, any worship folder will have a "prayer list." While the list might include names of missionaries or pastors, it is usually dominated by prayer needs for physical concerns. I can't help but wonder how the church would change if, instead of praying for physical bodies that have a limited duration, the congregation would pray for souls to be saved and lives to be transformed.

Library shelves are filled with books on prayer—its biblical imperatives, its ecclesiastical history, its psychological fulfillment, and its miraculous accomplishments. Even more books have been written on the "how-to" aspects of prayer. Having read thousands of pages on the nature, effect, and mechanics of prayer, I must say that the best advice I've ever received is from Nike: *Just do it!*

Outreach

The Spirit distributes gifts within the body of Christ, and the Scriptures tell us that different people possess different gifts. We all know people who, within their own experience, have the gift of exhortation, or the gift of wise counsel, or the gift of healing, and certainly there are those who have a gift for evangelism. And while many don't possess the gift of evangelism, we are *all* called to be "witnesses" to what Christ has done.

Far too many pastors preach convincingly of the saving power of Jesus and then conclude the sermon with the admonishment, "Go out there and change the world," but they never offer a word of instruction of exactly *how* to change the world. The world is changed through "evangelism" or "outreach": the personal sharing of our experiences and our faith.

Among all the Sunday school classes offered and mid-week services held, the healthy congregation has an ongoing instruction of the sharing of faith. There exists a wide range of curriculum on the subject, from simplistic approaches such as the Four Spiritual Laws to more complex models such as Evangelism Explosion. Many larger evangelical congregations have developed their own instructional materials.

My personal experience is to teach people to write down their personal story of salvation from three simple vantage points: "Before I met Jesus," "How I met Jesus," and "Since I met Jesus." Then I teach them to "edit" that story down to the quickest telling and end it with a question that will lead the other person to talk about his or her own life.

Evangelism is a gift, but being a witness is the responsibility of every believer.

Governance

I believe that the level of health—or illness—of a congregation can be observed by attending a church board meeting. One can see if the board controls the pastor or the pastor controls the board. One can see if the board is micro-managing the activities of the staff or if the staff is not being accountable to the board. One can see if a single strong person or family decides which projects get accomplished and how they are done. One can see if the church is governed for health and growth or stifled and hindered in accomplishing its mission.

A healthy trend as of late is that more and more congregations are shifting from a multi-board to a single-board system. Multiple boards often operate at cross-purposes to one another and have a tendency to function as "management" committees, getting mired down in details that require additional time to bring everyone to consensus, and are often composed of those willing to serve rather than those who have a useful level of expertise.

Boards that serve as "trustees" are often reluctant to part with funds for budgetary items outside of their own assignment. The facility is seen as something to be preserved rather than a means of outreach and ministry. The church van or bus is an expensive item to be maintained while other ministries are under-funded. Instead, a single board that has oversight over the spiritual and financial aspects of the congregation can focus on both.

As a congregation grows, the professional staff of the church also grows. When that occurs, the thinking of the board must also evolve from a "management" approach to a "governance" approach. If the staff includes an educated minister of Christian education, for example, then a board of Christian education, a Sunday school superintendent, or a Sunday school secretary may not be needed. When a congregation has a business manager or executive pastor, the board should not have to review every contract for cleaning supplies or cell phones.

A governance-style board creates fiscal, ethical, missional, and legal parameters within which the pastors are free to act, and then holds them accountable for their actions. This is how most successful businesses operate. In other words, if a pastor initiates a program that complies with the mission of the congregation, is funded within the confines of an approved budget, has met whatever legal and ethical requirements may exist, and doesn't put the church at risk, the board should approve and support it, as well as hold the pastor accountable as a part of the evaluation process. Crucial in this or any corporate process is the understanding that proper communication must occur before, during, and following the project.

Discipleship

Pastoral work involves not only the teaching of the elements of the faith, including how to reproduce the faith in others, but keeping records of the individual growth and development of congregational members. In the waning days of the twentieth century, my associate pastor, Jim Sirks, presented me with a list of decisions that our congregational members should make—things such as to attend church, to receive Christ, to be baptized, to participate in a discipleship group, to join a ministry, to practice stewardship, to lead another to Christ.

Looking back on a lifetime of full-time pastoral ministry, I have come to realize that the wise pastor enters into any new pastorate with Christian education materials that speak to these critical decision-making points in the lives of believers and should be adaptable to the size and culture of the congregation. Just as Acts 2:42 lists the elements of church growth (fellowship, discipleship, worship, ministry, and evangelism), so should the pastor understand the culture of the congregation and develop methods of enabling church growth in these areas.

Program Oversight

A successful pastor develops administrative and oversight skills to manage the programming of the congregation. The key component to this is development as a leader. Leadership is a trait rarely spoken of and rarely taught in seminaries and Bible-training schools. It involves strategic planning and the development of long-range goals that are then integrated into vision-casting: keeping the thinking of the leadership and the focus of the congregation on "big picture" items. Every program should be part of the overall strategy of the congregation in fulfilling its mission. One aspect of keeping the vision before the people is to ask the question, "What are we celebrating?" What gets celebrated is what is regularly put before the eyes of the congregation.

In my last ministry assignment before retirement, our church experienced great growth, especially during the first seven years of my pastorate. We grew from eighty parishioners to over 400. Since then my colleagues have often asked me, "How did all that growth happen? What was the magic formula?" Actually, there wasn't a single secret, but a formula of several behaviors—all of them counter to the traditions of the congregation, yet all of them consistent with the gospel; all done consistently week-in and week-out; all done deliberately and intentionally; all aimed for a common goal.

We reduced the number of meetings, reduced the number of boards, and changed how the single board conducted itself, so congregants could have time to participate in outwardly focused ministries. We reduced the length of our worship services, so visitors could feel comfortable about knowing when a time of worship would start and when it would end. We strengthened our ministry to children—from crib-room care to upper elementary, involving the best of our people, whom we trained and equipped. We developed policies and procedures so that everyone could operate under the same code of expectations. In other words, we stopped thinking like a small church.

We stopped asking anyone in the congregation if there were any announcements. It was the job of the pastor(s) and staff to stay abreast of the activities of the church. As staff, we put the necessary information in the worship folder and pointed it out to the congregation. We stopped making "small group" announcements to the whole church. We stopped taking prayer requests during the worship service. We found that we couldn't control how much time Brother John or Sister June would take to tell the entire story of their cousin's gall bladder surgery. Worship was not the place to tell those stories anyway. We stopped taking "special offerings" for a myriad of good and noble causes, and placed those causes in our budget. This helped our people become better stewards of their money.

I believe the Church—the capital "C" Church—was not purchased with Christ's blood for potluck dinners, and pages of prayer requests for bodily healing, and worship services that don't worship, and two-hour meetings to decide how to spend $75. I believe the Church—the capital "C" Church—exists to transform lives. And to accomplish that, a lot of "small church thinking" and traditions have to change.

Pastoral Care

Carlisle Driggers, a pastor in the same town where I once served, offered me a word of counsel: "When there is congregational trouble, increase pastoral care."

My response: "That seems too simplistic."

He explained, "There's nothing simplistic about it. Pastoral care is more than making visitation to homes, hospitals, and care facilities. And it's more than listening to people's complaints about the church, the board, or the pastor. Pastoral care is understanding the basis of the congregation's needs—emotionally and spiritually." Driggers then said four words that I have repeated often: "Hurt people hurt people."

Through the years, I have found great wisdom in those words. And, yes, there is nothing simple about it. A woman who lost her child is plagued by memories of every harsh word she uttered to that child. A man who failed at business lives with the regret of every financial error he made. Our pews are filled with hurting people who have experienced abortions and addictions, who have estranged relationships with their children, parents, and in-laws. Mention the word *regret* in any conversation (or sermon) and mental images race across people's minds of errors of words or actions.

I took Carlisle Driggers' advice. I increased pastoral care. Yes, I visited more, and moved more slowly through groups of people during times of fellowship. I listened to words of complaint, but I also asked more questions. I came to understand the regrets, pain, and hurts that my people were living with every day.

Preaching Competence

It is important that the preaching moment be planned and prepared for. A hastily composed outline coupled with forty-five minutes of rambling edifies no one and brings shame to the gospel. As preachers who are also pastors, we must be committed to approaching the pulpit zealously. And it's not always easy.

A key to accomplishing any task is time management. A pastor's time must be managed, and especially so when it comes to sermon preparation. Any single sermon is, I believe, best composed by following a correct formula of several different periods.

READING TIME

Each day of a pastor's life should include a time for reading, and not just the Bible. There is a wealth of illustrations and thoughtful insights that can be found from biographies, histories, and even meaningful novels. Nothing can broaden and deepen our thinking more than reading. These perceptions can find their way into the preaching moment.

RETREAT TIME

It has long been a practice of mine to spend two or three days each quarter in retreat. Different pastors call it different terms and use it in different ways, but for me it has always been about sermon preparation. I use the time to plan my preaching schedule for the entire year. Marking off special events, vacations, holidays, and guest speakers, I plan to feed my people from exegetical, topical, and biographical means, being sure to address felt needs, preach my way through a book of the Bible, cast vision to the congregation, promote stewardship, and call others to faith. Subsequent retreats flesh out specific sermons in greater detail, coupled with a great deal of writing—sometimes in outline form but more frequently in prose, creating syntax that will be refined later.

WRITING TIME

For me, I've used three blocks of time during each week for sermon preparation. The first part of that time is used for writing. Here a skeleton of a sermon begins to take on flesh. Illustrations are added, and appropriate quotations are found.

For other sermons I'm working on, I will use the time to edit, to pare down the excess fat, to consider which illustrations and quotes might best be used in another sermon at another time. In this process, I'm editing not only for content but also for time. A long and rambling sermon filled with unnecessary frills does no honor to the message or the messenger, wastes the time of the parishioner, and hinders the Spirit in bringing conviction to the hearer.

Conclusion

When I was in college, a number of ministerial students were obsessed with choosing a "life verse"—a single verse or passage to serve as a mission statement for their lives. I began scouring the pages of the Bible to find one for me, but nothing seemed to fit—at least nothing that I felt God was specifically designating to be "my" mission statement. Several years later, during a regular meeting with my mentor, he spoke into my life and into my heart in a way that made perfect sense to me, and I immediately knew my "life verse" and a detailed direction for my life. It's found in Luke 16:10–12 (NIV): "Whoever can be trusted with very little can also be trusted with much, and whoever is dishonest with very little will also be dishonest with much. So if you have not been trustworthy in handling worldly wealth, who will trust you with true riches? And if you have not been trustworthy with someone else's property, who will give you property of your own?"

At first that seemed almost counter-intuitive, but as I pondered it a moment, the truth became apparent. A person who would waste time on television is a person who would waste time in the office. A person who is undisciplined with his or her eyes is a person who is undisciplined with his or her hands. A person who can't be trusted with your money is a person who can't be trusted with your wife or husband. Trustworthiness with a small amount of money (or supervision, or authority, or any assignment) is an indicator of how a large amount will be handled.

There are times in everyone's life when the "big things" seem so mammoth and so imperative that we are tempted to lose our focus on the importance of the "little things": to do justice, to love mercy, to walk humbly (Micah 6:8). Justice, mercy, and humility are "little things" that have huge ramifications.

About the Author

Rev. James Leslie Sparks has served in full-time ministry since 1970 in Indiana and Michigan. He holds a Bachelor of Arts degree from Anderson University and a Master's Degree in Counseling from Olivet Nazarene University and has certifications from the Bethel Bible Series, Evangelism Explosion, and CoachNet. He has written for numerous periodicals, including contributions to *Vital Christianity*.

Rev. Sparks was a founding partner in Awakenings LLC, a private counseling ministry. He helped found the Samaritan Center in Munster, Indiana, and has served on the board of directors and chaired the General Assembly of the Church of God in Michigan. At his retirement in 2013, he was named pastor emeritus of the North Avenue Church of God in Battle Creek, Michigan. Since that time, he served as regional pastor of Southwest Michigan for the Church of God and held several interim pastoral positions before being named church health minister for the Church of God in Michigan. He and his wife, Susan, live in Battle Creek, where he enjoys reading, writing, and training his horse.

4. A Layperson's Perspective

by Edward Eddy

I am a preacher's kid, but in a non-traditional way. Both of my parents were preaching ministers. However, to my knowledge, neither of them had ongoing ministerial roles within the church body we attended. Primarily what they did was deliver sermons occasionally. I still have a vivid memory of one particular sermon my mother preached at the Third Street Church of God in Kansas City during a gathering of area churches on a Sunday afternoon. Her mantra for that sermon was, "Jesus was a young man!" My dad, who could neither read nor even write his own name, prepared his sermons by having us children read selected passages to him. His memory was remarkable as he quoted or paraphrased from Bible passages we had read sometimes two or three days earlier.

My mother and I shared a love for the Psalms, and this book is still one of my favorites from the Old Testament. Sometimes I gathered our neighborhood playmates to "cottage meetings" in our living room. I would lead the singing while my mother spoke and made the appeal to become followers of Christ. Some of my friends were convicted during those gatherings because they told me later that they were "scared" when the Word was delivered. A few of them joined our church fellowship for a time.

Our parents sometimes invited ministers to our dinner table on Sunday afternoons. On those occasions, my mother prepared some of her most sumptuous meals. She had a lot of experience cooking every day for our large family.

A Closer Walk

"Blessed is the man that walketh not in the counsel of the ungodly.... But his delight [his joy, his greatest satisfaction] is in the law of the LORD; and in his law doth he meditate day and night" (Ps 1:1–2, KJV). When asked to deliver a Father's Day sermon two years ago, I focused on the character of David. I studied the first Psalm to gain insight into the question of why God described David as a man after his own heart (1 Sam 13:14). It is no revelation to students of the Bible that God loves to use weak, flawed people. This man committed adultery and murder! However, David possessed many qualities that merited God's approval. Among them were:

- his absolute faith in God;
- his love for God's Law;
- his awareness of who God was;
- his suppliant petitioning;
- his heartfelt repentance;
- his gratitude;
- his humble spirit;
- his increased obedience and maturity.

God looked into the core of David's being and found him to be a man after his own heart. David's finest hour occurred when he restrained the desire to get even with his father-in-law for trying to kill him. Instead, he placed the matter in God's hands. As a result of this singular quality, God laid the mantle of excellence upon him.

These challenging truths caused me to seek a closer walk with the Lord, which has resulted in a deeper, more dynamic relationship with him and a more fruitful life. Because of the many times I have repented for falling short, my Bible almost opens automatically to Psalm 51. But I am grateful that it also easily opens to the litany in Psalm 107: "Oh that men would praise the LORD for his goodness, and for his wonderful works to the children of men!" (v 8, KJV). After fifty-six years of marriage, I continue learning how better to apply these principles in our spousal relationship.

One salient point stands out from studying David. Now that I'm living in God's bonus years—ten years beyond three score and ten—gratitude for all of God's mercies is my unending response. I can change my behavior, but only God can change my heart. Through confession, by allowing the floodlight of God's love to shine on my faults and shortcomings, my heart is cleansed and renewed. Then I can relate more authentically to others. I'm learning to love people the way God does.

My issues do not define me in God's eyes. It is the condition of my heart that concerns God most. "When I am weak, then I am strong" (2 Cor 12:10, NIV). Living by the servanthood model of Christ has moved me from a life of doubt and brokenness to a place of peace and contentment. I am no longer hesitant to express godly love toward people. Granted that not everyone will receive it as intended, but I am committed to heeding the second greatest commandment with its many iterations throughout the New Testament: "Love your neighbor as yourself" (Matt 22:39, NIV).

Authentic Leadership

I teach online courses in leadership for Mid-America Christian University in Oklahoma City. The assigned textbook, *The Leadership Challenge: How to Make Extraordinary Things Happen in Organizations* by James M. Kouzes and Barry Z. Posner, has been relevant to my own Christian journey. The authors assert that, although Jesus is recognized as the greatest leader who ever lived, his strategy of leadership ran counter to conventional ideas. The book lists five practices deduced from the servanthood model of leadership personified in Jesus Christ:

1. *Modeling the Way*: Operating out of high values, ethical behavior, and honorable ideals

2. *Inspiring a Vision*: Encouraging others to create and commit to a shared vision and goals

3. *Challenging the Process*: Encouraging innovation to address needs and aspirations among constituents

4. *Enabling Others to Act*: Collaboratively building a climate of trust that brings about competence and confidence

5. *Encouraging the Heart*: Affirming others by celebrating their accomplishments and genuinely expressing appreciation for their abilities and aspirations

The engine that drives the whole process is *agape* love expressed by word and deed in all interpersonal relationships. I believe the pastors under whom I have served endeavored to demonstrate some, if not all, of these five principles. In my opinion, many of our ministerial leaders model the kind of behavior that reflects a God-called ministry.

Jesus gives each of his followers gifts and talents, working through these to make himself alive within the church. He equips us to love and serve one another, bringing unity to his kingdom. "The undeniable diversity found in the Scriptures does not obscure the fact that we are dealing here with one [primary biblical truth]: a coherent account of God's purpose for the world and for each of us. God-called preachers…are *stewards* of this amazing Story. There is great joy in such a stewardship, but it brings a burden as well. Story-stewardship implies a unique calling, a divine commissioning, a holy accountability, and a distinctive demeanor among those who would handle it well."[1]

After modeling the way by working on oneself, the second step is doing the right thing. At times, I have witnessed novice ministers parroting the words and mannerisms of their mentors. While the desire to emulate one's mentors is commendable, naked imitation comes across as inauthentic, especially if the listener is familiar with the original. I learned very early in music ministry to find my own voice—to discover my unique message and manner of expression.

My Perspective

Here are some observations, concerns, and convictions I urgently wish to share from my perspective as a layperson:

1. *It is imperative for leaders to have a vision, one in which hopes, dreams, and aspirations are doable and can be embraced by the congregation's constituents.* This kind of vision is powerful if fueled by a godly passion that captures the allegiance of fellow sojourners. Once vision becomes clear, the next step is to enlist others by listening deeply for clues to fashion a genuinely shared goal. The aspiring leader would do well to remember that innovations and initiatives involve risks. The servant-leader is prepared to persevere in the face of adversity, an attribute called "psychological hardiness." It means being unperturbed by negative opinions and circumstances, even a willingness to suffer and to make sacrifices. The servant-leader doesn't spend too much time assessing aptitudes. Rather, he or she uses the resources at hand, all the while seeking the Spirit's direction to fill the strategic roles necessary to accomplish the goal.

2. *Many of our local churches fall short when it comes to practical strategic planning.* Congregations would do well to enlist expertise from outside sources, if necessary, when setting goals and planning major projects. There is a beginning, a middle, and an end to the planning process. The process includes counting the cost, anticipating non-financial resources needed—time and personnel— and potential challenges, the "what-if's" that surely will surface along the way. In-stage assessment and a post-mortem are equally important to determine the effectiveness of the effort and address unmet expectations and misunderstandings that may have cropped up. Desire and passion do not replace the need for expertise in assessment. If major projects and undertakings leave a congregation and its leader estranged from each other, there probably was some vital aspect of planning missed or unattended in the process.

3. *The most positive body life experiences I have had were characterized by a climate of trust between leader and congregation.* It takes commitment and time to achieve this. Sometimes what looks like hesitancy to get on board with the new leader is caused by the need to dissolve long-term allegiance to the previous leader— not because people have reservations about the new leader. Separation from a long-term and well-loved pastor is akin to losing a loved one through death. The feeling of loss is tangible. Some of the hardest-working members within a church body need time to let the separation process take its course. Godly

love and allegiance, though required, is not indiscriminately extended, nor is it easily forsaken. A wise servant-leader discerns and respects this. If he or she takes offense at such seeming reluctance, there could be trouble ahead for the pastor-member relationship.

4. *Another critical area of leadership involves something that is difficult for many leaders—admitting mistakes.* Sometimes a leader attempts to move too quickly, perhaps because he or she perceives the urgency of the need. Even so, it takes a large dose of humility and courage to admit when you are wrong. If a leader is unaware or unwilling to take small steps to build confidence among the more reluctant constituents, trouble ensues, especially from informal leaders within the body, even if they seem benign. Sometimes zeal overrides good judgment. But the act of showing one's vulnerability by admitting error is usually rewarded with increased trust and credibility. I learned this lesson painfully as a college dean supervising twenty-something students who always voiced their reactions frankly.

5. *Finally, the servant leader enables others by fostering collaboration.* Wise leaders give their power away as Christ did before he left the earth. By so doing, the cause becomes the business of all the leader's constituents. Collaboration builds trust. Everyone has an area of giftedness in the body. When leaders develop character and confidence in people, they too lead out of a servant's heart. The degree to which one is able to build trust and give power away directly affects the kind of organizational life grown. Such leadership encourages the hearts of the people. "Leadership is not conferred. It's earned."[2] Service and sacrifice are redemptive. The best thing leaders can do is invest in the long-term development of people and churches that can adapt to changing circumstances, prosper, and grow.

A Hunger for God

In this final section I want to share some wishes—things that would have helped me to overcome as a struggling young Christian. These expressed desires are not meant to be taken as one-size-fits-all. The spiritual culture and worship manner of some congregations may preclude some ideas, and I respect that. Neither do I wish to imply that these "what-if's" are not addressed anywhere, but this is a call for a broader, more intentional and inclusive application of them in local and national church life.

As a young man, I aspired to serve on the mission field, but could not find access to the opportunity. I received no response from written inquiry to the Church of God international headquarters, neither did my pastor seem to take my aspirations seriously. I wish I had received more helpful feedback, even if it were, "This is what you need to do to prepare," or, "This is not the right time because"—some helpful advice that addressed my fervent desire to serve God in this way. Even though my request may have been misguided zeal, still, I needed help with processing my aspirations.

I wish I had received the kind of professional help I needed in my spiritually formative years. I shared deep-seated personal issues with every pastor under whom I served, but did not get help beyond basic spiritual advice. As I matured from being a high-maintenance young Christian to a more mature, internally motivated one, my pastor continued to relate to me as if nothing had changed. I could have resolved some of the pain of my issues with professional help. Likewise, how I wish my pastors, who provided effective counsel in my early years, would have recognized the maturity I gained under them. We could have avoided some of the friction that resulted from miscommunication because my interpersonal competence had evolved. Sometimes I felt demonized in my role as leader for speaking as an equal on procedural matters. I never was one to be publicly confrontational, rather I was a team player with strong leadership skills and expertise in my field of endeavor.

I wish pastors and worship leaders could feel comfortable breaking with the traditional order of the worship service at times when the Spirit moves in a special, palpable way. Sometimes the Spirit is powerfully manifested through a song, a prayer, or a praise report in the midst of a worship service. Discerning worshippers recognize such a special move, but the designated worship leader may miss it and move on, intent on fulfilling his or her responsibilities (not to belittle that concern). When this happens, those sensitive to the move of the Spirit later comment on the missed opportunity for a harvest of souls and victories or the opportunity to edify the body through a time of praise. Leadership seems reluctant to allow this because someone may abuse the opportunity or respond inappropriately. On the occasions when I, as worship leader, attempted to do this, it was not well received.

I have witnessed missed opportunities to cull additional spiritual help from a particularly powerful spoken word. Some parishioners who sensed the Spirit's move expressed the need to discuss the principles set forth, perhaps in a small group setting immediately after service. We usually could tell when it was needful, as we were leaving service feeling hungry for more of what we just experienced. We were not interested in critiquing the sermon; rather we wanted to embrace more fully the principles set forth by exploring what they looked like in practice. Learning is enabled if accomplished before the natural process of forgetting details sets in. This may, in fact, be happening somewhere, but I never had such an opportunity aside from sitting briefly with a few friends after service. I'm aware of the common response to such desire—a caution about not staying on the mountaintop, but I believe we also can miss out if we leave before the Spirit is through. God's timing is not necessarily consonant with ours.

Another wish I have is that when local congregations or our national organizations are seeking conference leaders, workshop presenters, and such, they would get references from more than one person, usually the individual's pastor. This is the same principle that pulpit search committees are advised to use. There is an untapped cadre of laity with gifts and skills who are serving locally but are overlooked by current recruitment methods at broader levels. Some pastors seem to be more willing than others to allow their constituents to have exposure beyond their local boundaries. To avoid using someone who may be inappropriate for whatever reason, local pastors and national church leaders could work together to develop procedures. Building the safeguards into the process, rather than leaving it to individual local leaders to give ad hoc consent, would avoid the unfortunate circumstance of overlooking capable and worthy individuals who could contribute significantly to the larger church body. Many capable parishioners are reluctant to market their skills within the church because they have been taught not to "toot their own horn," whereas they are quite willing to do so in the secular arena. Higher-education professionals are encouraged to update their résumés and curriculum vitae listing every single thing they have ever done and to present them at appropriate times. A related suggestion: conference planners could send out a call for topics and presenters which then could be approved by the process suggested above. Local, state, and national church organizations could provide the framework and the catalyst for this process.

Another aspect of leadership practice I wish pastors would adopt is to be more intentional in affirming and celebrating the small victories and accomplishments of members. I have found pastors to be very good at admonition, correction, and accountability, but slack with positive feedback and affirmation. People who serve unreservedly need to know that they are not taken for granted. I gave my all doing double and triple duty serving in several ministries simultaneously—Christian education, youth work, music ministry, Sunday school, etc.—for many years. I have no regrets about serving the way I did because it was a labor of love. In hindsight, I would have appreciated an occasional token acknowledgement from leadership along the way. What I really needed was not monetary compensation, but appropriate and timely affirmation. For lack of it and for other reasons also, I suffered from burnout, which adversely affected my personal and family life. It seems to me that in full-time ministry, the individual is addressing two of the three most important spheres of adult responsibility—work, family, and church, whereas the lay volunteers have to juggle all three, separately. When I was volunteering at the church every evening, familial responsibilities went lacking.

Finally, a healthy church is one where the Word is being preached, one with a strong cadre of supportive members using their gifts to the benefit of the body, one where a majority of members are thriving spiritually, where all age groups are getting their spiritual needs met, and where there is a harvest of souls occurring. I am blessed to have enjoyed that kind of fellowship in most congregations in which we have been members. Not everything went smoothly all the time, but we always overcame the internal and external obstacles by being prayerful and receptive to the leading of the Holy Spirit. One of the best definitions of excellence that I have encountered was written by Harold M. Best. Building on his understanding of Philippians 4:8 ("whatever is true, whatever is noble," NIV), Best defines excellence as "the process of becoming better than I once was…not to become better than someone else is."[3] Indeed, the Scriptures admonish us not to compare ourselves to others. None of us attains excellence with every attempt because we are flawed creatures influenced by mitigating circumstances and interpersonal challenges. Excellence in God's sight is not an event; it's a process, and it's not measured by earthly standards.

Conclusion

The ministers in the churches I have been a part of have helped me have a closer walk with the Lord. I am grateful for their authenticity, their vision, and their hunger for God. Effective pastors and ministers challenge and prepare their parishioners to grow and serve. They are sensitive to the Spirit's leading. They enable their people to use their gifts and skills beyond the local church. And they are intentional about celebrating the victories and accomplishments of the people in their congregations.

Recommended Books

Christian Reflections on the Leadership Challenge by James M. Kouzes and Barry Z. Posner

Is This All There Is to Life? Finding Wisdom for Life in Ecclesiastes by Ray C. Stedman

The Leadership Challenge: How to Make Extraordinary Things Happen in Organizations by James M. Kouzes and Barry Z. Posner

Music Through the Eyes of Faith by Harold M. Best

Stewards of the Story: The Task of Preaching by James Earl Massey

Wasting Time with God: A Christian Spirituality of Friendship with God by Klaus Issler

About the Author

Dr. Edward A. Eddy, PhD, MA has early memories of sitting under Pastor Walter Grizzell's thunderous "voice of God" calling the congregation to repentance at the Freeman Avenue Church of God in Kansas City, Kansas. As a youth, he thrived under the spiritual nurturing of local ministers such as Harmonia Wilson, Otis Walker, Goff Young, and Anna Mae Young. Later as a young adult, he was privileged to sit under the teaching and preaching of Pastor Sethard Beverly and his wife, Saundra. Years later, he and his wife, Joyce, moved the family to Chicago, where they were privileged to participate in the social causes and outreach ministries of Pastors Claude and Addie Wyatt, along with Rev. Willie T. Barrow and Dr. Alvin Lewis.

Dr. Eddy worked as a teacher in elementary and secondary public schools before spending thirty-three years as faculty and/or administrator at higher education institutions. He continues to serve the Christian community with presentations on worship and music ministry. He enjoys spending time with his thirteen grandchildren.

1. James Earl Massey, *Stewards of the Story: The Task of Preaching* (Louisville: Westminster John Knox Press, 2006), xi–xii.

2. James M. Kouzes and Barry Z. Posner, *Christian Reflections on the Leadership Challenge* (San Francisco: John Wiley & Sons, 2004), 123.

3. Harold M. Best, *Music Through the Eyes of Faith* (San Francisco: HarperCollins, 1993), 108.

5. Nurturing Your Own Family

by David R. L. Stevens

So, you feel that God is calling you into ministry. That part of his leading, you are not having difficulty with. However, there is another part of the call that is bothering you a lot. What about your young family? You have a beautiful spouse, a set of five-year-old twins, and a baby on the way. During your seven years of marriage, you have managed to get your degree and now there has come an offer for you to pastor First Church.

All of the above would seem to suggest that God is supplying for you and bringing multiple blessings. A major concern in your mind, however, is with the expectations spelled out in the First Church contract. The calendar events listed are stacked so aggressively that it is obvious there will be very little quality time for you to devote to your family. Added to that, you have already signed on to be the keynote speaker for several out-of-town conventions. You want to be faithful to God's calling. Since you were quite young, you have felt the hand of God on your life. Why now all these confusing thoughts in your mind?

Isn't all this attention and recognition a sign that God is already pleased with your life? I have always believed that what God assigns, he blesses. Where the problems arise is when we try to add our plans in with God's plans. It may have to come down to a raw acceptance of this fact: When God commissions us, he has already sanctioned the blessings that go with that commissioning. It is a good and wholesome idea to sit down and try to separate out what God wants from what we want. I will admit that this is not always easy. However, until it is done there is always going to be a mental and spiritual conflict. Sometimes it will end up being physical as well.

God is a master planner and provider who favors us, based on sovereign will, according to his plan. Confidence in what God is doing, never smugness, is called for on our part. I have heard some people say that God needs certain people to bring his plans about. I think it is more accurate to say that God desires or chooses to place some of us in a plan that he is developing—it's more like we have an opportunity to participate in a designed blessing. We are not special to the task, as if there is some greatness that we possess. No, our involvement is not based on a merit system! Only God knows why we are being chosen for a particular event, assignment, or task.

The Pastor-Spouse Relationship

In all of this, we must consider the love relationship between pastor and spouse. They were united at a marriage altar with an expressed commitment, understanding, and agreement that they would be partners for life. We understand a pastor's love for the Lord, but a great deal of that commitment to God should be acted out in the relationship with his or her spouse. They are partners, or should be partners, in every aspect of life. This includes business, ministry, family values, child rearing, and a host of other things.

Very early on I realized that loving my wife Dorothy called for me to learn who she was through and through. I had to become a student, studying this wonderful gift God had given me. I had to learn all of the deep mysteries that made her who she was. I learned to put aside many of the generalities and assumptions that would benefit me on the surface. I had to begin changing the life-long love affair I had with myself. I knew that I had a gem, but began to learn how to polish and secure that rare gift. One of the first things I discovered was that even though I tended to want to be alone with my own thoughts, she wanted to be with me in them. Selfishness had to give way to companionship. Often, she just wanted to know what I was thinking about. I never had to do that before. But we are becoming the partners we promised to be; that is God's plan, and it is good.

Just like in every other couple's relationship, there have been things that have been challenging to us. But God has always been good to us. We try to never forget that we signed up to be partners in and for life. This does not mean that we agree on every single point, but what we do agree on is that we must work together. We both want to do the right thing in the best possible way. *Let's try to find the best way* has been our approach. Husbands and wives in ministry need to come to grips with their differences.

Pastors and Their Children

Many pastors become misdirected in ministry, failing to maintain a proper family focus. I think there is a simple statement that gives us good perspective: "Family first." Many Christian homes could have been saved from destruction had they established this principle up front.

I think about families with children. Carelessness on the part of the pastor can cause casualties, jealousy, and feelings of abandonment, neglect, and general hatred for the church as an institution. Mistrusting God has sometimes resulted among our children because those answering the call of God put their families last.

It is interesting that Jesus made the following observation in a situation that may be unrelated but still illustrates the general principle of seeing and doing: "Very truly I tell you, the Son can do nothing by himself; he can do only what he sees his Father doing, because whatever the Father does the Son also does. For the Father loves the Son and shows him all he does" (John 5:19–20, NIV). There it is. Children observe their parents and tend to react to what they see. It is hoped they will follow the positive and pleasing things they observe, but we know it could work both ways. Yet, it would not be unusual for children to decide, even vow, to not have what they view as negatives included in their future lives.

I was listening recently to a story a man shared about his disappointment after following a famous pastor and then finding out it was all just words. This man dropped out of the church and became a very vocal critic. It works the same way with our children; they are affected not only by what is said but by what is actually done—or not done.

The ladies in our congregation have subtly reminded me more than once that their eyes are on their "First Lady" and how she is treated. I think that not-too-subtle hint is aimed toward me, though communicated in a kind manner. My love and respect for my wife, my life partner, must be demonstrated in such a way that it registers in the minds of our children. Whether or not we are specifically aware of it at any time, our children are watching us for sure.

We once attended a wedding reception with our youngest son, his wife, and their children. After asking our ten-year-old granddaughter how she liked her new school, we sat in amazement as she responded, "Well, there is a lot of drama." She proceeded to tell us of a situation in which one of the young people in her group exhibited some "inappropriate behavior." She then said, with the savvy of a much more mature and aged person, that her intentions were to move on from this girl. We were so impressed with how well she expressed herself, and her knowledge of right and wrong, in a mature, confident manner. This has got to be an example of some parent power rubbing off. Yes, our children are watching!

Knowing the Way

In God's Word, I find two extremely strong and helpful mandates in Proverbs 22:6 (KJV), which states, "Train up a child in the way he should go: and when he is old, he will not depart from it." Clearly, there is no option here. We must first train up our sons and daughters, which calls for some dedicated work by the parents. There is no license for a part-time service agreement. I have heard of some men in the past who felt it justified to go off and evangelize the world while the "little woman" stayed home and raised the children by herself. This is preposterous! Somehow, they ignored or were ignorant of the Word of God.

First Timothy 5:8 (NIV) tells us, "Anyone who does not provide for their relatives, and especially for their own household, has denied the faith and is worse than an unbeliever." So how in the world could someone be so enraptured by going around telling others about the life-changing power of Jesus Christ while at the same time neglecting his or her family?

I realize that we don't have the ability to save anyone, and this includes our children. I certainly want every one of my family members saved. Salvation is offered to all, but the choice is up to each individual. My responsibility is to provide the best spiritual, social, and physical environment I can. God gives us a chance to glorify him by way of the family, and we must do all we can to prevent sacrificing this precious opportunity. Loving one's spouse is certainly where it must begin.

I want to return to Proverbs 22:6 and an important phrase that is often overlooked there. Just what is "the way a child should go"? Understanding this phrase helps us to find the deeper meaning of the passage. I don't believe these words are just poetic writing; rather, they indicate that each child is different in nature. There is more for me to do with my children than just the general training task. I must put in the time to know each of my children beyond the surface. Even if someone feels the call of God to be available to the world, home and family must occupy the first position. I cannot see God sanctioning a ministry any other way.

Wrath or Anger?

Added to all this is the wisdom Paul gave us in Ephesians 6:4 (KJV): "Fathers, provoke not your children to wrath: but bring them up in the nurture and admonition of the Lord." We must understand that when a passage such as this is addressed to fathers, it is holding mothers to the same standard. If we try to somehow change the importance of the principle along gender lines, we weaken it. Let me try to help us clear up handling gender-directed Bible passages. When something is first addressed to fathers it is setting fathers as the initial target, with the expectation of mothers following that same standard. Of course, the same would be true for fathers when mothers are targeted.

Now let's look at two other important words from Ephesians 6:4: *provoke* and *wrath*. Some have taken this part of the mandate out of context by recommending a no-discipline approach to child rearing. God is not proposing that we raise our children with no discipline. Without discipline, nothing much could be accomplished except chaos. Think of our world without discipline. But what this passage is strongly suggesting is that there is a definite line not to be crossed. *Provoke* is an active word and can have devastating results.

What is the "line" we should not cross? I think there are two parts to consider. First there is a general line, one that comes from plain old human decency. This line should be honored when dealing with any human being, regardless of gender and especially age. I say this because some folks feel that children don't count when it comes to treatment, but this is wrong thinking. There is a general line, and next there is, in my opinion, a personal line that goes back to our earlier discussion about parents having to put in the time to learn their children; we also need to train them in accordance with the will of God using methods of training appropriate to how each child learns best. We should be aware of a general line based on our humanity, and then of an individual line based on each child's personality.

When our children were growing up, I lost my temper one day and yelled at one of our boys, "You are lying!" Well, he went to pieces. I will never forget his hysterical appeal: "Dad, I have never lied to you in all my years; how could you say that to me? I am not a liar!" He was absolutely right. In all of his years we had never known him to say something untrue; he was committed to being a truth teller. My careless words certainly were provocative. I had to repent to my son and to God for that one. I should have known better.

Isn't it interesting that Ephesians 6:4 forbids provoking our children to wrath but not provoking them to anger? There is a difference. Anger can come and go, but wrath is different. Wrath carries with it an ugly depth factor. Words such as *vengeance* and *hatred* and the holding of deep grudges emerge when we think of the word *wrath*. It is the planting of deep seeds of hatred or bitterness. Sometimes when negative acts of vengeance are carried out, we incorrectly say the person was very angry. In reality, it would probably be more accurate to describe these acts as wrath. As parents, we must be concerned about our disciplining not being done in such a way that it plants seeds of bitterness in the hearts of our children.

Planting Positive Seeds

Let's be honest. There are people who want nothing to do with the church, or with Christian ministry, because of some powerful negative seeds that were planted in them during their childhood. Often it was from perceived neglect, the feeling that their relationship with their parents had been displaced by the parents' ministry efforts. This may only be true in the mind of that child and never intended by the parent, yet the onus is still on that parent or those parents. It can be a tough call, but we must do everything possible to avoid providing negative seeds that can be planted in our children.

One of the great hymns of the faith indicates that it takes time to be holy. I think we could apply that same principle in loving our families. As pastors, we must take the time to share the love for God and his work that captured us. We must learn our children individually, taking the time to pour faith and satisfaction into them. We must let them find ways to join in helping others, let them know how much their input is valued, and let them know that they are in our hearts and never pushed to the side. How else can our children see the church and ministry other than through the view we give them? Even in trying to explain the call of God upon our personal lives, it must be done with great care so that our children don't develop a reluctant spirit against God himself. Until they are able to see for themselves, they will see through us.

It is interesting to me that, even though our children are fully grown with families of their own, I feel I have to be careful how I relate matters happening in the church to them. I don't want them to get a negative view of something that might sow seeds of wrath.

Speaking in Love

Since we have talked a great deal about what our families see, I want to mention also what they hear. I believe we should always speak the truth in love. This means that great care must be taken about what comes out of our mouths. I remember hearing one old preacher referring sarcastically to having the saints over for dinner. He was not talking about sitting down with them sharing a meal. Rather, he was talking about them being on the menu. We know that the saints are just reformed people who are at various stages of the reformation process. Some of them embrace the ministers who serve them with a spirit of gratefulness and honor. On the other hand, there are those who feel that their mission in the church is to make us better. Their cantankerous spirits, coupled with ungodly behavior, just push us to an unwelcomed place.

It is sometimes tempting to bring such frustrations home with us in spirit—home, where we can feel free to liberate ourselves and say openly what we would really like to say to such people. No, my fellow workers, never make the mistake of blowing off steam in front of your children. It may feel good at the time, but it is unhealthy and hurtful. After taking it to the Lord and seeking his help, it will be all right and you will be able show up for work in the morning with a smile on your face.

As we serve God in ministry, he will prepare us to carry the load of unwarranted attacks and abuse and help us to eventually recover from it. But our children don't have that capacity. We cannot unwittingly allow seeds of discord to be planted in the fertile soil of their hearts. At this point, they are helpless. We must protect them!

Conclusion

The family is given to us for a blessing. It is a great opportunity to develop a close, intimate community. It is a place of love and laughter and support. We should never allow anything to interfere with its value and purpose. Let your life be a life of principles. If along the path you make a mistake with your family—and you will—be quick to admit it and do whatever you have to do to make it right.

About the Author

Rev. Dr. David R. L. Stevens is the senior pastor of Christ Center Church of God in Philadelphia, Pennsylvania, where he has served for nearly fifty years. He was ordained in 1969 by the Church of God and received his Doctor of Divinity degree in 1981 from Jameson College in Philadelphia.

Dr. Stevens currently serves as chairman of the Delaware Valley Pastor's Fellowship and as chair of his district's credentials committee. He is a professional artist and marriage counselor and has authored nine books on the subject of marriage and relationships.

Dr. Stevens is married to Dorothy Grimball Stevens. Together they have four children all actively serving in the church, and ten grandchildren. Dr. and Mrs. Stevens co-founded the Second Wind Second Mile Ministries, now known as Sound Marriages, with the motto, "Because we love God and his people!" They have travelled nationwide doing seminars, presentations, workshops, and private counseling sessions. See www.davidstevensbooks.com for more information.

6. Why Every Pastor Needs A Pastor

by David Hall and Keith Hall

Serving as a state minister allows one the unique privilege of becoming a part of the lives of other pastors. The life of a pastor is unlike any other in the local congregation, and the responsibilities of serving are very demanding. One of the most often reoccurring concerns coming from pastors is their prayer life.

The Priority of Prayer

Prayer must always have priority for pastors and ministers to thrive in their called field of service. For many of these individuals, their prayer life is either not as strong as they would like, or it is not as much of a priority as it once was. For some there arises a feeling of a lack of power. This feeling can hinder pastors in every aspect of ministry—leaving them with doubt and fear in their ability to fulfill their calling.

For others struggling in their prayer life, their thoughts go to measuring their own effectiveness and realizing that prayer is no longer the first thing they turn to. This can become a very difficult place to be in ministry, with guilt and doubt replacing confidence and courage. The pastor may begin to feel guilty for not spending enough time in certain ministries of the church. He or she may begin to wrestle with how much time to spend in the office or how little time was spent in sermon preparation. These feelings of guilt will cause pastors to question everything about their calling and ministry.

It is a difficult thing to be a pastor with a struggling prayer life and no one in your local congregation to talk to for fear of reprisal. In such times, pastors need another pastor. They need someone to hold them accountable, someone to try out new ideas on, someone who will offer a challenge without being dismissive or demeaning.

Accountability: an Issue of Trust

The main focus for accountability between those pastoring and those pastoring pastors is trust. In times past, to hold a certain position was to hold a level of "expected" trust. We now live in a culture where trust needs to be earned and accountability within the life of a church is sometimes difficult to find. For most pastors, there is a desire to befriend a member or members of their own congregation and for some, a level of success in this area is achieved. However, many pastors discover how hard it is to trust individuals within their own congregation, and this can result in unexpected difficulties in the pastorate.

The most painful aspect of a pastor's ministry can be the struggle with issues of accountability and who can be trusted. It is important that a relationship of trust and accountability be firmly established, allowing for a pastor's prayer life to flourish in this atmosphere of trust. Trusting relationships with other pastors can bring growth for the pastor and also for his or her congregation.

If pastors have the confidence that there is someone they can trust and who prays for them regularly, then they in turn will see their personal prayer life strengthened and will begin to trust more in God's leading and less in themselves to "fix" all their church problems. This can help to combat feelings of guilt that arise in ministry—feelings that are common among all pastors. Guilt over not spending enough time in certain ministries of the church includes the areas of office hours, sermon preparation, and visitation, and also not spending enough time with the family. While some may not think "family time" is necessarily a ministry concern, try to separate the two into different schedules within any given week and you will quickly discover how intertwined they are.

There is great comfort in knowing that someone is praying for you. There is a measure of trust and accountability that is absent when that experience of mutual prayer does not occur among those in the ministry.

We can imagine the reaction to Jesus' words when he told the gathered crowd on the shore of the Sea of Galilee, "Love your enemies and pray for those who persecute you" (Matt 5:44, NIV). It must have been a shock that such a command would be given for an all-inclusive level of prayer and love. This same measure of love would inspire Paul more than once to directly charge believers to pray for one another.

If Christ commands us to pray lovingly for those we might regard as our enemies, then why would we ever neglect to pray for those who are our brothers and sisters in ministry? Paul understood the relationship between accountability and trust and the role prayer has in strengthening such a relationship. As much as he encouraged the church to pray for one another (Eph 6:18), he also asked them to pray for him (Rom 15:30). Prayer for one another in ministry is both biblical and beneficial and serves as a vital ministry for all who are called to pastor.

The Primacy of Prioritizing Time

When pastors fail to organize or when they dislike the discipline of time management, they fall into a pattern of never having enough time in life and ministry. They often experience times of being ill-prepared and frustrated over things not getting completed. This can become a difficult issue in the life of ministry, stalling the effectiveness of pastors and the congregations they serve. With no one to answer to on a daily basis, a pastor who fails to practice effective time-management will often fail to plan. If such pastors tend to procrastinate, their schedules become inundated with events, emergencies, and the desires of certain boards, committees, and even individual congregants. This creates an "accountability shift" in ministry. A careful look at a pastor's schedule will give clues about what serves as the measure of accountability for him or her.

Good time management prevents one from becoming accountable to those from whom there is no positive feedback. Such misdirected accountability means that success becomes measured by events, emergencies, and energy-draining individuals. These people will many times hold a pastor accountable for things that have nothing to do with ministry. When you combine the lack of a faithful prayer partner with the stress of ministry and the desires of the congregation, it isn't any wonder that pastors are leaving the ministry.

In a pastor's relationship with other pastors, it is good to ask about their prayer life but also how they are managing their time. Perhaps we do not see time management in the ministry to be as important as prayer. We may not ask to review a pastor's day-planner, but there are other ways we can offer counsel and share time-management skills.

Many pastors feel that there are not enough hours in a day to accomplish all that needs to be done. However, encouraging someone to get up an hour earlier each day, though simple in thought, can prove valuable in practice. The key will be in how one chooses to use that hour. If you desire to intercede regularly for others, why not do so with an extra hour each morning? The benefit of this hour, particularly if spent in intercessory prayer, can have such a Kingdom impact that you may feel led to increase it to two hours before long, and you may end up with more free time throughout the week.

God gives us all the same amount of time each day. We need his wisdom to use that time effectively and efficiently. Who better to discuss issues of time management with than the Lord himself? Think of the challenge you could offer to someone in ministry to consider praying briefly about each event scheduled for the day. If we could honestly pray for one another's schedules, think of the impact it could make in effective ministry practices.

Jesus stressed the importance of one-on-one discussions and how they bring healing and help and even hope into every relationship. He pointed out an important principle for us to apply: "Truly I tell you that if two of you on earth agree about anything they ask for, it will be done for them by my Father in heaven" (Matt 18:19, NIV). It may take time to develop a relationship that allows one to compare datebooks, but the investment would yield positive results.

Ministry can be draining, and a full schedule does not necessarily mean a productive ministry. A time-management skill that is often overlooked is "break time." It almost sounds wrong to take a break when there is so much to do, but much more could be accomplished if you would take breaks. Pastors are notorious for working without breaks. After all, since they are doing the Lord's work, wouldn't taking a break violate their ministerial call? The answer is *no*, and the breaks need not be long. Taking regular breaks can help you maintain your focus. Whether it's going for a brief walk, calling a friend, throwing a baseball around, or something else, it can give you fresh energy for the rest of the day.

There is great value in developing good time management skills. There is greater value still in sharing those skills with others, as it instantly increases the value of those skills. When pastoring other pastors, we may want to consider asking not only about their prayer life but also about how they are managing their time.

The Importance of Personal Relationships

Pastors need to have someone close enough to ask the hard questions about temptations, sorrows, and failures. Equally, pastors need someone to celebrate the victories, accomplishments, and personal triumphs in their own lives, in the lives of their families, and in the congregations they serve. If every pastor could have such a confidant, this would keep many from moral failure, leaving the ministry, or losing their families through divorce.

As long as discouragement is a part of ministry, pastors need a ministry friend. Discouragement can come from a lack of response from the congregation, a vote going the wrong way, a goal not being reached, a decrease in attendance, conflict from people opposed to ministry changes—the list never seems to end.

If you focus on the negatives, Satan will fill your life with one problem after another. You need someone to give you balance, someone to coach you and pray with you. A pastor really needs a pastor! It is vital when working with other pastors to develop personal relationships. But sadly, this subject is often avoided by those who stand in greatest need. Pastors will many times hesitate to share personal details when talking with other pastors, instead giving information about their vocational life that may not reflect what is taking place with them personally.

The development of personal relationships is key for a pastor to have a healthy ministry in the local church. The pastor's mental, personal, and spiritual well-being depend on the quality of personal relationships he or she has, and one of those relationships should be with another pastor.

If your desire is to come alongside another pastor and be a resource and partner in ministry, you need to understand this person, his or her culture, and the way this person relates to others if you are going to have any positive impact on his or her life. When we have "connection moments" with other pastors, we need to see these as wonderful opportunities to build upon. These moments cannot take place unless time and trust are exercised regularly in developing a relationship. Time and trust are the two issues that require the greatest amount of attention. There is always the temptation to seek out shortcuts to time and bypass earned trust with assumed trust. This is mistake, as it causes a breakdown in a relationship that is very much needed.

It is important for pastors to continuously attend to and nurture their relationships with other pastors. Perhaps the two greatest challenges in maintaining these close personal relationships are neglect and properly dealing with conflict. It is important to become aware of what neglect and conflict can do and seek to be proactive in addressing them.

Pastors, we really do need one another! None of us were meant to go this journey alone. We are a needy people, and there are those who need us. They need us to spend time with them, and in turn we need to give our time to them. They need for us to be present in their lives and ministry, and in turn we need to make ourselves available to them. They always need a listening ear (even though they may not ask), and we have that ear. We have it within us to give to others, and we need to receive from them. No matter what side of the equation you find yourself on, relationship flourishes in this environment of giving and receiving.

In building personal relationships with other pastors, one great piece of advice is to start small and push through the awkwardness. I used to disdain so much small talk in the church until a seasoned pastor reminded me that most people have to wade in the shallow end before they'll try swimming in the deep. Except for the most extroverted among us, getting to know people is challenging. But Rome wasn't built in a day, and neither are friendships. Keep your hand to the relational plow.

Facts are important when sharing with and supporting other pastors. But don't just ask about the test results and the medication and the next doctor's visit. We must be willing to talk about fears and worries and doubts and joys and hopes and disappointments.

When you pray for and with another pastor, follow up. I always find it amazing (and encouraging) that so many people will pray for me in a time of crisis or pain. I find it doubly amazing when those people circle back later to tell me they are still praying and ask how I am doing.

The Scriptures make it clear that "in Christ" the Spirit of God has been poured out and now we all are priests to one another. First Peter 2:9 (NIV) says, "You are a chosen people, a royal priesthood, a holy nation, God's special possession, that you may declare the praises of him who called you out of darkness into his wonderful light." Here Peter drew from some descriptive phrases used for Israel in the Old Testament. As the new Israel, God's chosen people—the church—are uniquely called to minister to one another. Perhaps this is the greatest reason to intentionally seek to develop relationships with other pastors.

As pastors and ministers caring for one another, we must have a good understanding of who we are what we are called to do. While we may like the sound of being a "royal priesthood," we should first understand that God chose us in our weakness and our inability to save ourselves. We need to remember that we ourselves needed help in the past, we still need help in the present, and we will need help in the future. This knowledge provides a strong sense of humility that may be seen by the world as a point of weakness but is, in fact, a source of strength—God's strength (2 Cor 12:9–10).

It will always be easier for us to listen to the needs of others and seek to help them and speak to their needs. Many pastors find this becoming their ministry focus and can become codependent on their congregations to the point where they become the "answer" instead of seeking "The Answer" together. A better result would come from our understanding that we need one another and need help from one another. After all, we are limited human beings. One needs only to sit in on the conversation between Job and God to draw that conclusion.

The question we must constantly keep before us, then, is, "How do we help one another?" Answering this question will serve to help us minister to one another and build relationships that provide help to all of us who need help.

Conclusion

Let us close this chapter with three words that will be easy to remember as we strive to help others. The words represent things Jesus did, and there is no better model than our Lord when it comes to pastors helping pastors.

First of all, Jesus intentionally *engaged* others. He was willing to make the first move. Surely he was motivated by his love for all and his willingness to extravagantly express that love to anyone. Engaging in conversation and initiating the conversation will require us to pursue others and engage them.

Some people have personalities that make it easy for them to engage people, while for others it is a difficult chore. For one, asking, "How are you?" may be very easy, while for another not so. Yet for those who find it an easy task, the temptation is to get the easy answer and move on to the next person. Whether this is a challenge are not, the greater and more important part is to go deeper.

We cannot become content with the pat answers and simple replies of an initial engagement, which is merely the "knock at the door" and serves as an opportunity to go further in the development of the relationship. You need permission to *explore* with questions that go beyond the surface and reach the heart. When you read in John 4 about Jesus requesting a drink, can't you hear him engaging the Samaritan woman at the well and intentionally exploring her need?

Engaging should lead to exploring and cause us to learn more about one another, which permits us to help one another. The conversation moves beyond "How are you?" to questions such as "What can you tell me about yourself?" This helps to identify the deeper heart issues, which strengthens relationships and builds the much-needed element of trust that leads to the experience of an *encounter* that will make an impact, allowing pastors to get help themselves and give help to those in need. With the woman at the well, an encounter took place between herself and the Living Water—Jesus Christ. We can offer the greatest help to other pastors as we engage one another, explore our shared needs and identify those places where we need support, and encounter the hope and healing of Christ together.

The beginning of this chapter spoke to the priority of prayer, and it is therefore fitting that we end at the point of prayer encounters with one another. Spiritual leaders stand in great need of being prayed for by their congregations and by other pastors. Time management is important and so is establishing personal relationships through engaging, exploring, and encountering. But if there is a priority that cannot be overlooked, it is expressed in Paul's words to Timothy when he admonished him, "I urge, then, first of all, that petitions, prayers, intercession and thanksgiving be made for all people" (1 Tim 2:1, NIV). All pastors need a pastor, and they need to know that prayer is being lifted up for them.

About the Authors

Dr. David Hall currently resides in New Port Richey, Florida, with his wife Delores and just completed an interim assignment there. Prior to that, he served as a regional pastor in Mississippi and Illinois. Hall has served on various national boards and committees for the Church of God, including the Ministries Council, the National Budget Committee, the Children of Promise board, and the board of trustees of Mid-America Christian University. He is also a trained SHAPE,

NCD, and CTI coach, along with serving the greater church as an evangelist.

Rev. D. Keith Hall resides in Mississippi along with his wife Elizabeth, where he is serving as the regional pastor. Before his current assignment, he served as a senior pastor for twenty-five years at churches in Mississippi, Illinois, Missouri, and Ohio, and as a youth pastor for four years in Kentucky and Ohio. He has taught as an online adjunct instructor for Mid-America Christian University and is currently serving as a coach with Leadership Focus, the national credentials training program for the Church of God.

PART II:

Specialized Perspectives on Pastoral Ministry

7. Bi-Vocational versus Full-Time Ministry

by Bartholomew Riggins

Many congregations of the Church of God and other church groups in North America are in need of more effective and efficient models of ministry. One prevalent challenge in urban, rural, and small towns is the lack of full-time professional ministry structures. This is especially true among many African American congregations. There are several factors at play, including:

- the lack of economic opportunities in certain urban areas;
- the limited number of professionally trained pastors available;
- the lack of sufficient economic resources to support a full-time pastor;
- general contentment in many places with the traditional church culture of having the pastor be bi-vocational;
- the tendency for churches in rural communities to be small.

The aforementioned factors have all contributed to the absence of an adequate church growth strategy and the lack of sustained services to nurture a congregation's potential, causing some churches to close their doors.

Churches that are open on weekdays as well as on Sundays can often reach persons and families who have not been raised in a church tradition. Additionally, the number of children growing up in single-parent homes is accelerating; concurrently, parents are becoming younger, and these "youthful" parents have a critical need to learn how to be parents. The drop-out rate from high school is on the rise, which negatively affects students' access to good jobs and economic advantages. Furthermore, the number of young persons who are arrested and sentenced to terms in jail and prisons is rising. The need for a caring church that has an active, available ministry to deal with those experiencing hardships is obvious.

Faith Chapel Church of God of Baton Rouge, Louisiana, was founded in 1948; however, I am the congregation's first full-time pastor. My emphasis in this congregation has been to increase the effectiveness of our organizational mission and provide a model for other congregations of the Church of God in the southeast region of Louisiana. My intent is to encourage local churches to develop a vision beyond bi-vocational ministry structures even if it seems improbable at the present time. Pastoral and lay leadership in local, rural, urban, or suburban settings should be exploring a plan to gradually move their congregations toward becoming full-time in ministry presentation.

I was given the privilege to introduce changes in the local church I now serve by moving our church from bi-vocational ministry to full-time ministry, and I have a strong passion for helping congregations develop strategies for accomplishing more as a "weekday" church versus a "weekend-only" church. I am hopeful that other churches will see the value of such a change. While our church is not the first African American Church of God congregation in the South that has moved from bi-vocational to full-time ministry, we are the first in Louisiana to do so. We hope to influence other churches to do the same. We also hope to share cooperatively with other full-time ministry congregations in this region of the South by learning from their strengths and weaknesses, their successes and losses, and to share our story and experience with them by serving other congregations as a mentor congregation.

Full-time ministry structures in local congregations will demand adequate salaries and benefits, and it can be difficult to think about such a move when money is tight. Nevertheless, it is necessary to underscore that regardless of economic conditions, local congregations of the body of Christ need to operate at an optimal level of ministry, and this is best accomplished when we plan to act through full-time ministry structures. It is becoming increasingly critical that pastors have the courage to invite local congregations into such a journey of paradigm shifting.

Historical Considerations

Because a congregation is in a small town or rural area does not mean that it should never aspire to being structured for full-time ministry. Most of the congregations that currently have bi-vocational ministry structures began with leaders who served on a "circuit" basis. The congregation could expect its pastoral leader to visit the church once or twice a month, alternating visits elsewhere at other times. Usually, the pastor would have two or more congregations that he or she would be overseeing. There are still areas and regional pockets of the Church of God, particularly in the deep South, that are yet operating under the circuit leadership structure; however, some other congregations have changed and have a minister who pastors only the one church and is available for ministry every Sunday during the month at that local congregation.

In some congregational cultures, the fact that the pastor is present and available every Sunday is equal to its definition of full-time ministry. Full-time ministry from a professional structural perspective, however, is not just about a single pastor being in service for Sunday ministry. The goal should also be to have the pastor available throughout the weekday hours to guide weekday ministries within the life of the church.

In the past, many of our churches lamented that they could not afford financial support for a full-time minister. The question today in some cases is not affordability, but rather, *What is the church's paradigm and mindset concerning the need for a full-time pastor?* It is my opinion that many churches in the South, especially African American churches that are located in rural and small towns, have been slow or even negligent in encouraging pastoral leaders to be full-time. Indeed, there are plenty of other churches representing different denominations in the same towns and rural areas that have managed to financially support a pastor for full-time ministry. There seems to be a greater awareness within some of the predominately African American denominations about the need for full-time ministry in the same small towns and rural areas where some African American congregations of the Church of God have long existed, yet continue to be bi-vocational.

Roles and Responsibilities of the Full-Time Pastor

It is possible that upon assuming the role of a full-time pastor, particularly in a congregation that is transitioning to full-time structures, the pastor may be tempted to have his or her hands on all aspects of church functioning. Over the long term, the approach of the micro-leadership model will stunt the growth of the church and also send the pastor into unintentional burn-out or permanent resignation from pastoral ministry.

It is vitally important that the pastor begin from day one with the approach of a larger vision of a *servant leadership* model. This type of leadership takes place when the church and pastor are willing to move into a sharing kind of mutual partnership ministry instead of a "lone ranger" type led solely by the pastor.

The following list denotes potential responsibilities for the pastor of a congregation that is transitioning to a full-time ministry model:

- Establish personal church weekday office hours four days out of the week, and of course a Sunday schedule.
- Establish weekly, quality family time with spouse and children.
- Work on intentional relationship-building with leaders and members of the local congregation as it relates to both ministry and life in general.
- Work on initial relationship-building community-wide with local business organizations and entities, city hall, educational alliances/school board, and ecumenical ministerial alliances.
- Establish regular physical fitness activities for personal health.

- Ascertain church-wide strengths, challenges, opportunities, and motivations as they relate to ministry within the congregation and also ministry to the community.

- Work on an ongoing process for shaping and re-shaping the vision for full-time pastoral ministry.

- Present a proposal or enhance any existing processes for activating a continuing, increasing number of willing workers by way of spiritual gifts surveys, coupled with implementation tools with regard to the results of those surveys.

Administrative Assistant Role

In a full-time ministry structure, good administration is vital to develop the effectiveness and efficiency of the congregation. Many church leaders with only bi-vocational experience find it difficult to provide the administrative leadership required. Every congregation needs to develop a master plan for managerial development if the church is transitioning from a bi-vocational status to a full-time ministry status.

Among African American Church of God congregations in the South, the current standard for administrative leadership often reflects the pre-twenty-first-century paradigm: secretaries, treasurers, bookkeepers, and financial secretaries, all of whom serve in a part-time capacity. My concern is not to belittle bi-vocational church structures, but rather to encourage a church to consider full-time ministry *whenever the resources are available.* My second purpose is to present information necessary to assist congregations to transition from a part-time to a full-time ministry structure.

A primary barrier to transitioning a congregation's mission focus is resistance to a paradigm change. Times of economic downshift can present an additional barrier to transitioning from bi-vocational to full-time administrative ministry structures, but the state of the national economy has not been the primary problem over the long term concerning changing church structures from part-time to full-time.

As it relates to African American Church of God congregations in the South, a combination of factors, including a misguided ministerial focus, has mired many churches in a continued condition of mediocre administration. Another problem that needs addressing is church office hours. For example, the ministry of the front office at the local church becomes challenging when office hours are scheduled on a part-time basis. In most cases office hours are maintained at bi-vocational churches during scheduled worship times.

At the Faith Chapel Church of God, prior to my assignment with a full-time ministry structure, the congregation had a part-time secretary as the sole person for front office administration. The responsibilities of the secretary included preparing worship bulletins, church-wide communications regarding ministry schedules, and basic financial record-keeping.

The pulpit committee at Faith Chapel decided in 2010 that new pastoral leadership would serve with at least one full-time administrative employee while the new pastor would be the first paid official serving forty-plus hours a week. Therefore, one of my immediate goals upon arriving to serve Faith Chapel was to hire an administrative assistant.

As Faith Chapel transitioned to a full-time ministry structure, there was some discussion about whether or not to hire the full-time administrative staff person from within the congregation or from outside of the congregation. While an insider already knows the "lay of the land," such a person can also be hesitant to try new things, and an outsider can bring fresh perspective and skills to the job. As the new pastor at Faith Chapel, I reviewed the current part-time secretary, her work efforts, her knowledge of office responsibilities and duties, and her relationship to the congregation. In this case I agreed with the approach of hiring from within, and while not all leaders in the church were in favor of this, it has become a welcomed success for our church.

Every congregation has a history and an existing culture, which must be identified and understood at the start of a new church administration. It would be foolish on the part of anyone to assume that a church culture begins when a leader arrives to serve. Transitional success with new leadership, both clergy and lay, depends on the meshing of an existing culture with new insights along with possible emerging modifications.

Lay leaders, clergy, and congregants must be committed together to review the historical path of a congregation to project a direction forward that can offer and encourage improved development. The culture of the church being under review in a collective approach to produce new direction is still a work in progress at Faith Chapel.

Job Description for Administrative Assistant

I worked with the full-time administrative assistant of the Faith Chapel Church of God to create her new job description. Following is an overview of what we came up with.

The purpose of the administrative assistant is to supervise and facilitate the day-to-day administrative operations of the congregation. This position requires professionalism, confidentiality, and exceptional oral and some written communication skills.

Under pastoral supervision, the administrative assistant is responsible for:

- supporting the vision, mission, ministry, and core values of the church;
- maintaining the church calendar and scheduling use of the facility;
- editing, producing, and distributing publications and bulletins for worship and administrative communications;
- maintaining files of official church records and documents;
- providing direct administrative support to the pastor, including calendar management, correspondence, and telephone messages;
- clerical support for the pastor and church committees;
- filing committee minutes and reports;
- editing, production, and dissemination of e-mail updates of events and worship themes;
- notifying pastors, church board members, lay ministers, and intercession ministers regarding church members who are hospitalized or disabled, births, deaths, weddings, and other events of church members and families of members.

The administrative assistant should be able to organize and administer information; follow through with details; have a good knowledge of computer hardware and software, including Word, Excel, Outlook, and church management software; and be faithful in attendance, with the ability to vary schedule when needed.

At Faith Chapel Church of God, office hours comprise a forty-hour workweek, Tuesdays through Fridays and Sundays, with the office being closed on Mondays and Saturdays. Although typical business-week office hours would run Monday through Friday, it has been my experience and observation that when a congregation has a limited staff, it is particularly important to design the work hours considering both the staff and the needs of the congregation.

The culture of church attendance in America is trending toward mass gathering at local fellowships during posted worship hours, but a variety of other ministries also happen during those hours, including discipleship, pastoral care, new member orientation, and financial, administration, and welcoming ministries. Due to the variety of ministries that occur during regular worship hours at the Faith Chapel Church of God, it has been considered necessary for the administrative assistant to count Sunday as a workday. This model has worked well for our parishioners; some members' schedules do not allow them to be on the church campus except for Sundays and Wednesdays.

Financial Considerations

The tithe is the optimum means and the clear biblical model for financing ministry through a local church, whether full-time or bi-vocational. Every full-time church should have the full support of members who are consistent tithers and regularly attend the church. The tithe should be the basis for determining the operational budget for a congregation's fiscal year. Though tithing in some church circles is viewed as an outdated requirement of the Law of Moses that does not apply to the church, I have advocated that it is important for both clergy and lay leaders to proclaim, model, and promote regular tithing yearly in the life of the local church. One way of assuring that the ministry of tithing is a core value of a local church's culture is by having a yearly series of discipleship teachings on the subject of tithing, whether in sermons from the pulpit or in a Bible study format.

At Faith Chapel, one of the vital emphases I have maintained is biblical teaching on tithing. Starting with pastoral leadership, tithing is practiced. Our church leaders and members are strongly encouraged to give a tithe to our congregation for the primary financing of Christian ministry. We teach our congregation that tithing was not only necessary during the time of the Mosaic Law but also before and after the giving of the Law. Abraham was a tither before Moses prescribed it (Gen 14:18–20). Jesus, who is the Messiah and came after Moses, also recognized the act of tithing (Matt 23:23).

Beyond the necessity of calling Christians to a practice of tithing, it should be emphasized that when the Christian tithes there is no loss of finances to his or her personal budget, but actually a gain. In fact, in Malachi 3:10, the people of God were instructed by God to test his generosity by tithing. As pastor, I teach that tithing does not decrease one's resources, but rather increases them, and helps to advance the work of God's kingdom.

The necessary goal for funding a full-time congregation is to provide for all of its basic ministries. On occasion a church may receive an unexpected large sum of funds; these funds could be deposited in a trust account instead of being immediately used just because the funds are available. The interest earned each year from trust fund accounts can be a steady stream of income for underwriting local ministries. Endowment funding helps when there may be a noticeable dip in tithes and offerings due to changes in the local economy. There may be persons within a congregation who have an interest in helping the church to establish an endowment fund. Other non-profits such as universities and charitable organizations have long employed the endowment funding method; churches should also take advantage of the opportunity to use this approach for maintaining their budgets and benefitting from financial resources perpetually.

Finally, never underestimate collaboration with other local churches in the ministry of sharing resources. More can be done when groups minister together than when they try to do everything alone.

Ministerial Compensation

When Jesus sent the seventy-two out to minister, he told them, "When you enter a house, ...stay there, eating and drinking whatever they give you, for the worker deserves his wages" (Luke 10:5, 7, NIV). During the time I was growing up in a pastor's family that served particularly among African American Church of God congregations in the deep South, it was almost taboo to even discuss in business meetings the pastor's salary or talk about whether or not the pastor should even have a salary. I am not suggesting that only African American congregations have had non-biblical thinking about pastors' salaries. Nevertheless, as an African American minister who has always been in congregations that were predominantly African American in membership, I am honestly reviewing some observations over a number of years.

Regrettably, I have observed how some congregations actually took the stance that the pastor should pay his or her way as the leader. Moreover, I have seen how pastors have been forced to live sacrificially for a great portion of their lives. "Salaries" were mere gestures in the form of occasional monetary tokens and occasional honorariums without any consideration for merited increases.

This kind of thinking is often voiced from persons in the pew who are concerned about cost of living for themselves, but neglect to think about a pastor's needs. As Jesus sent out the seventy-two, he made clear that they were indeed worthy of whatever wages they received as a form of payment in ministry.

Conclusion

Full-time ministers and pastors should be intentional about avoiding self-gain and being lured into a false notion that the ministry is about them. The ministry is never about the minister. The person who serves in ministry is an instrument of Jesus Christ. If the pastor's focus is primarily on self, he or she can become greatly demoralized when things go awry. Add self-centeredness to lean circumstances and there is a clear reason why many ministers bail out each month, with some never to returning to Christian service. Selfishness can cause a minister to forget that it is in Christ, not in himself or herself, that all things are held together (Col 1:17).

Moving a church to a full-time ministry model can help the church serve more people, increasing the effectiveness of the congregation's organizational mission.

I would encourage local churches to develop a vision beyond bi-vocational ministry structures. It can be done, and God will bless your efforts.

About the Author

Rev. Dr. Bartholomew M. Riggins has served as senior pastor of the Faith Chapel Church of God in Baton Rouge, Louisiana, since July 2011. He was previously pastor of Light of the World Community Church of God in Shreveport, Louisiana. Bart and his wife, Joy, have two sons, Joshua and Titus.

Bart serves as the vice-lead coach for SHAPE (Sustaining Health and Pastoral Excellence) for the Church of God in Louisiana. He is also the lead stakeholder pastor for the Gardere Initiative in East Baton Rouge Parish and the greater Baton Rouge area, a board member for Connections Ministry in Baton Rouge, chairperson for the pastoral health team for the Church of God, and a board member for the Ministry Retreat Center of the Louisiana Church of God.

Pastor Bart's most valued mandates for life and ministry are loving the Lord; loving and keeping personal family strong in the Lord; loving people, including the people of God and those who need to know God; and loving Kingdom work.

8. Reflections of a Female Pastor

by Adrienne Holmes

I've seen the lightning flashing,
And heard the thunder roll;
I've felt sin's breakers dashing,
Trying to conquer my soul;
I've heard the voice of Jesus,
Telling me still to fight on;
He promised never to leave me,
Never to leave me alone.
—Ludie Day Pickett, "Never Alone"

The words to this song, and the assurance of Jesus never to leave me alone, are what have kept me in ministry and pastoring for over twenty-five years now.

My calling into the ministry was somewhat like that of Jeremiah and Samuel. In Jeremiah 1:5 (NIV), God told Jeremiah, "Before I formed you in the womb I knew you, before you were born I set you apart." My mother told me the story of how I was named by God before I was born. She said my father had prayed for a girl, and back in those days there were no sonograms or ultrasounds to let you know the sex of a child. My mom said that one night while she was lying in bed, God wrote my name around the top of her poster bed, like an airplane writes in the sky. She said nobody was naming girls Adrienne in those days. They were giving them names such as Helen, Myrtle, and Bertha, not Adrienne. I thank God for my name!

First Samuel 3:2–5 (NIV) tells about Samuel's call from God: "One night Eli, whose eyes were becoming so weak that he could barely see, was lying down in his usual place. The lamp of God had not yet gone out, and Samuel was lying down in the house of the LORD, where the ark of God was. Then the LORD called Samuel. Samuel answered, 'Here I am.' And he ran to Eli and said, 'Here I am; you called me.' "

One morning while lying in my bed in the house of my youth, I heard a voice calling my name. I got up and went into my mother's room and said, "Yes, you called me?"

My mom said, "No, I didn't call you." This happened at least three times. The second time it happened and I asked Mom if she called me, I even went to the window and looked out to see if anyone outside was calling my name, but no one was there.

After the third time of getting up and going to my mother, I laid back down and the Spirit of the Lord spoke to me, saying, "The Spirit of the Sovereign Lord is on me, because the Lord has anointed me to proclaim good news to the poor" (Isa 61:1, NIV).

I thought to myself, "Me, preach?" and I put the thought in the back of my mind. However, the Lord kept bothering me and bothering me, so I went to my pastor and told him what God was calling me to do. After letting him know that God was calling me to preach, he told me to go back and pray about it. I went back, prayed, and sensed the same calling: "The Spirit of the Sovereign Lord is on me." I went back to my pastor a second time and a third time, and he sent me back a second and third time telling me to go and pray. I went back, prayed, and got the same answer.

One Monday night while sitting in a ladies' meeting at church, the teacher said, "If you are telling the pastor that God is calling you to preach, you can forget it, because he does not believe in women preachers."

"Wow," I said to myself.

The next time I went to my pastor and let him know I was called to preach, he told me to go teach Sunday school. I did go to teach in Sunday school, and in every class I was preaching. After class, people would come up to me and say, "Do you know that you are preaching?" I would tell them that I couldn't help it.

The superintendent of the Sunday school sat in one of the classes I was teaching and said to me, "Do you realize that you are preaching?" I told him the same thing, that I couldn't help it. So they moved me to the preschool class, where God began to use me to convert three-year-olds and four-year-olds to love Jesus and follow Jesus. Soon the pastor realized that I was preaching and not just teaching in the class, and they changed my designation to "substitute teacher" so I would only be teaching classes when the regular teacher didn't show. And guess what? They would utilize all the other substitute teachers but never me, in an attempt to contain what Jesus was calling me to do.

When God has a calling on your life, God will make room for your gifts. So if I was asked to be the mistress of ceremonies for a program, I preached. If I was asked to welcome the visitors in church, I preached. Every speaking opportunity that was afforded me, I preached. God had called me to preach, and I preached.

The "Good Ole Boys"

The late rock-and-roll singer James Brown wrote and recorded a song called, "It's a Man's Man's Man's World." By and large, preaching and pastoring have historically been a man's world. I am not accepted in the preaching community by most male pastors; many of them are intimidated by me.

I know Jesus, I live my life for Jesus, I know my Bible, I don't compromise his gospel, I am a gifted preacher, I am well educated, I have an earned doctorate from the Anderson University School of Theology, God has blessed me with several churches that are not store fronts, and I am known in the community for my love for God and his people. So therefore the "good ole boys," the male pastors, will not allow me into their circles, or their pulpits. This is fine with me because as long as God is for me, and is continuously blessing me, it doesn't matter who is against me.

I must admit that at one point in time it did hurt me to be ostracized because of my sex, my gifts, and my calling. But God assured me that he promised never to leave me alone, and he hasn't. I respond to the insults, put-downs, and rejection as a woman pastor by looking at the doors God has opened for me and the blessings he has bestowed upon me.

For a time, I attended a college where women were not allowed to take pastoral classes, but I signed up for these classes and took them anyway, including the preaching class. When it came time to graduate, the college administration discovered that I had earned a Pastoral Studies degree and was not going to allow me to walk. But one of my professors insisted that I had earned it and that I had the right to participate in the graduation ceremony. The college ended up giving me a degree that said "Bachelor's of Religious Education" instead of "Bachelor's of Pastoral Studies." The church where I first pastored burned and we were victims of a scam while I was studying for my doctorate, but through it all I graduated with honors and even wrote my dissertation on the topic, "Forming a Community of Prayer."

During the time I was pastoring two churches, I was given the title of Bishop, and I am often ridiculed by others for the title. The "good ole boys" always protest by saying, "How can a woman be a bishop when 1 Timothy 3 talks about a man being the husband of one wife? Are you the husband of one wife?" For a long time I struggled with that passage, even while serving as a pastor, and I prayed to God because God is the one who called me in the first place.

I said to the Lord, "I keep coming up against this passage. What does it mean? Am I not supposed to be doing what I am doing?"

Here is what God said to me: "Paul did not need to address his words to a woman here because a woman could only have one husband at a time in that culture. Men such as Solomon and many others in Bible times had more than one wife, and those other wives and concubines caused them to worship idols and led to their demise."

When my church burned and the "good ole boys" talked about me, again I went to God and said to him, "Lord, am I not supposed to be in ministry or pastoring? Look at what happened to me!"

God spoke into my spirit, "Adrienne, if you weren't supposed to be pastoring or ministering, I would not have given you this church before the building burned." Each time the "good ole boys" came against me, God stood for me.

In a lot of circles I am not recognized as a pastor, minister, or preacher because I am a woman, which is a put-down and an insult, but I know who I am and whose I am. I was Adrienne before I had any of those titles and as long as you recognize me as a child of God, with a message from God, that's all that matters to me. We cannot allow insults and put-downs to keep us from our call.

There have been times when I walked into a church wearing my collar, or attended a funeral led by a male, and have been asked not to enter the pulpit. I was once invited to preach at my sister's church, but the men in charge directed me to a podium on the floor. When I stood up to preach, I paid honor to whom honor was due and then told the congregation, "Thank you for the podium because I don't care where I stand to preach—as long as I get the opportunity to preach, I can preach from the back door!"

Time and time again, in church after church, the men have spoken down to the women so often and so forcefully that we have taken a back seat and are sitting on our gifts. But I say to you as the captain said to Jonah on the ship, "What meanest thou, O sleeper? arise, call upon thy God" (Jonah 1:6, KJV). God will hear you and make room for you in the vineyard because the harvest is plentiful but the laborers are few.

I ignore the insults, the put-downs, the out-of-context Bible statements, and the rejection of the "good ole boys." I say to all women, if you know for sure that God has called you, God will be with you in everything that you do for him and for his people.

God's Blessings in Ministry

As a woman pastor, I have been blessed over and over by God. I have had the blessing of:

- being able to lay with a girl in the street who was hit by a car, consoling her and leading her and her family to Jesus;

- preaching and leading Bible studies in both men's and women's prisons and leading numerous persons to Jesus;

- placing a child of a prison inmate in the home of one of our members so this child would not end up in the system. The child is now fourteen years old and is doing well;

- being a comfort to a mother who had lost her newborn infant to death after three days of life;

- opening a daycare that houses up to 130 children on a daily basis and teaches them the songs of Zion, the ABC's of the Scriptures, the Lord's Prayer, and the pledges of the Bible and the Christian flag, and gives them their first foundation as to who Jesus is and can be in their lives;

- teaching kindergarten, teaching children the fundamentals of reading phonically instead of using "sight words" so they can read anything that they see;

- adding a motherly touch to the gospel and preaching it so that God is understood as a loving, merciful, kind, forgiving, and saving God;

- pastoring one of God's churches where no one can tell me where to stand when I preach, and what areas I am prohibited from preaching in;

- training young men and women through an organization I created called "The Youth Corps," teaching them skills to mow grass, cut weeds, and do small maintenance jobs where they can earn money on their own—and while doing so, instilling the love of God in them so that some of them have led their families to Jesus;

- counseling with numerous people from all walks of life, leading some to Christ and dusting my feet of others;

- praying for children on their way to school, standing on the corner praying for the community, and then in the midnight hour praying for our city, state, and government officials and the needs of our world;

- being able to preach at the National Association of the Church of God convention in West Middlesex, Pennsylvania, and around the world by Internet;

- after threatened eviction from our facility and being turned down by numerous lending institutions, being able to acquire our current church building for our congregation and ministries.

I have been truly blessed by God in my ministry and my pastorate. My greatest joys in what I do for God are my successes for his kingdom. The song "Only What You Do for Christ Will Last" talks about the fact that we might build impressive churches and huge skyscrapers and conquer past failures, but only what we do for Jesus will last. Everything that I do, I do to bring glory and honor to God because I have given myself away so that he can use me.

My Vision as a Pastor

As I start each day with prayer, I ask God to allow Abounding Grace Church of God to be a place where his heart is, where the Bible is taught, the gospel is preached, sinners are saved, backsliders are reclaimed, Christians are encouraged, people are loved, and his name is edified, magnified, and glorified and Satan is horrified, petrified, and terrified. This is my main vision for the church overall. I want God and his Holy Spirit to always dwell in Abounding Grace and be the leading force of everything we do. My vision for the church is to always be able to take Christ beyond our Sunday gatherings by caring for the people in the community. I want us to be a missional church, a church with a focus on serving God and serving his people by providing needed monetary assistance, clothing, food, and a place for the homeless.

Locally, I would love to build onto the church facility to have the room to provide more services to the community, things such as a Christian elementary church school from infancy up to grade six and a women's Bible college geared to teaching and training women for ministry. Many young people in our society live in abusive homes or suffer from abusive relationships. I would love to start an organization that offers counseling to these young people and teaches them that even though they may have been raised in such an environment, it is not cool and it doesn't have to be their lot in life. I want to teach them that love doesn't hurt.

Globally, I would love to preach around the world, encouraging women to stand up and use the gifts that God has blessed them with.

Conclusion

> The world's fierce winds are blowing,
> Temptations are sharp and keen;
> I feel a peace in knowing
> My Savior stands between;
> He stands to shield me from danger,
> When earthly friends are gone,
> He promised never to leave me,
> Never to leave me alone.
> —"Never Alone"

In all that I have experienced in ministry and pastoring, God has never left me alone.

Women, God is calling you—not just to cook for the pastor's anniversary, serve in children's church, or make beautiful bulletin boards to grace the vestibule. God is calling some of you to the gospel ministry, to teach the Word and to preach the Word. How can they tell us that we as women can't preach or teach when a woman was the first to carry the word, deliver the word, and then preach the good news of the resurrection? Women were the last ones to remain at the cross and the first ones to show up at the tomb, and Jesus himself gave them the mandate to go tell that he had risen.

Women, stand up and preach!

About the Author

Rev. Dr. Adrienne Holmes is the mother of five adopted children, the grandmother of twelve, and the great-grandmother of one beautiful little princess. She is the proud pastor of Abounding Grace Church of God in Indianapolis, Indiana, where she has served for over twenty years. She is also the owner of Breath of Heaven Christian Bookstore, which is currently the only Christian bookstore in Indianapolis.

Adrienne first heard God's call to preach as a teenager and persisted through significant opposition to complete her studies and share God's Word with others. She was the first black woman to graduate from the Anderson University School of Theology with a Doctor of Ministry degree. It was from her doctoral dissertation that her book *Forming a Community of Prayer* was published.

Adrienne's life motto is, "If I can help somebody as I pass along, then my living will not be in vain."

9. Reflections of a Retired Pastor

by Robert O. Dulin, Jr.

High on my "bucket list" is the desire to invite fifteen to twenty pastors, who have served the same congregation for at least twenty consecutive years, to dialogue together about this question: *If you could start your pastoral ministry over again, what would you do differently?* I am in my late seventies and have served three years as an associate pastor in Kansas City, Kansas; two years as a pastor in Cincinnati, Ohio; five years as a full-time national program staff person in Christian education; and thirty-five years as a pastor in Detroit, Michigan. I am now retired from pastoring but continue to serve as an on-call funeral home chaplain and as regional pastor for the Churches of God in Southeastern Michigan.

After reflecting on fifty-plus years of ministry, there are at least five things I would try to do differently.

1. I would give more time and attention to commending people for what they do well and for what they try to do well.

While I commended people for what they did well, I did not do it often enough. More importantly, I did not spend enough time commending people for what they *tried* to do well.

There is much to be said for "process praise"—i.e., commending effort as opposed to giving praise based upon outcome. If people do something well, or if they try to do something well, and then feel it is ignored, they will probably do it less well the next time or perhaps not do it at all, thinking that no one cares. If I could start my ministry over again, I would give more attention to highlighting the things people do well or try to do well.

Commending people is an art, perhaps a gift, to be perfected. It involves the ability to recognize what has been done, as opposed to withholding a compliment because of what remains to be done or because of what was poorly done.

Commending and appreciating people for their effort is an art that requires *tact* and *emotional honesty*. Merely commending people who fell short of doing what they tried to do borders on being ingenuous, particularly if the commendation is not followed with recommendations for ways to improve upon their efforts.

Commending people for effort when effort falls short of the desired outcome needs to be followed with guidance on what they can do to do better next time. This involves much more than giving negative or positive feedback. It involves giving *accurate feedback*; feedback that encourages, that helps people to see and discover what needs improvement as well as what they can do to improve.

While it is right to hold people to high standards, we should also seek to commend people in ways that help them achieve high standards. This involves commending people not only for their achievement, but also for what they did to achieve high standards. A full and complete commendation focuses upon both a successful performance as well as upon what one did to achieve a successful performance. For example, commending a student for receiving an "A" on a geometry exam is a laudable thing to do. It is even more laudable to commend the student for what he or she did to get the "A" (assuming the grade was not the result of cheating). Commending the student's attention to hours of study, to memorizing formulas, to practice—this will encourage the student to study more and to give due diligence to memorizing additional formulas in anticipation of getting "As" on future exams. Commending someone who performed an outstanding, extraordinary piano recital should also include commending this person for the long hours spent practicing for the recital. Excellence is not achieved magically. Excellence is the result of discipline, practice, study, and hard work—all of which deserve commendation.

Additionally, providing people with the resources necessary to help them achieve is a critical component of commending and encouraging people to achieve. Recommendations for improvement should be accompanied with the resources necessary to implement the recommendations. If the recommendation is that one should attend a forthcoming workshop on leadership development, and the person does not have the funds necessary to pay the registration fee, the recommendation will more than likely fall on deaf ears.

2. I would be more aggressive in removing incompetence.

Or, to put it more positively, I would be more assertive and strategic in helping volunteers find their place in ministry. People's competencies and gifts should indicate what services volunteers are best suited and equipped to render. If I have learned anything from watching the television program *American Idol*, it's that some people cannot sing! Therefore they should not be allowed to sing in the choir, even if they are faithful and want to sing in the choir. Obviously, there are countless other examples. Faithfulness and a passion to serve are only two of many necessary qualifications for leadership and for rendering effective volunteer service. In addition to faithfulness and commitment, those who serve need skills and competencies—abilities that are measured against a standard.

Those who serve, whether as paid professional staff members or as volunteer staff members, must have the skills and competencies necessary to render effective service. Additionally, they need to evidence a hunger and thirst and a willingness to improve their skills and abilities. They must be teachable and open to advice. When this is not the case, it behooves the pastor to help such persons accept their deficiencies and give themselves to doing things more suitable to their competencies.

While I know this to be true, I have found it to be more easily said than done. Working with volunteers you wish you could fire and live to tell about it comes with the territory of being a pastor. During my years of pastoring, I found few things more frustrating than having to work with volunteer underperformers who, though faithful, had reached the point where they demonstrated the "Peter Principle"—that is, the point where they had reached their highest level of competence and were on the border of incompetency.

If I could start my pastoral ministry over again, I would:

- write job descriptions for all volunteers, job descriptions that communicate clearly and explicitly what is expected of those who volunteer to serve;

- make known the process for evaluating volunteers' performance and for holding volunteers accountable;

- be more intentional about putting in place a program for the ongoing recruitment, training, and management of volunteers;

- lead the congregation to secure a part-time staff person or volunteer to coordinate and oversee the church's volunteer personnel and service.

3. I would spend more time helping my critics and enemies find healing for their damaged emotions.

There is at least one person in every congregation who seems gifted to throw stones at others. Such people seem to enjoy throwing stones and rarely miss their intended targets. More often than not, their primary target is the pastor.

People who throw stones tend to be motivated to do so by carrying into their present unresolved issues from their past. The saying, "Hurting people hurt other people" is true. One of the dimensions of pastoral ministry is to help *all* people—even our critics and enemies, the difficult people who throw stones—to find healing and move beyond their past debilitating issues, hurts, and disappointments. Trying to help difficult people who throw stones find healing for their damaged emotions is akin to the challenge involved in daring to hug a porcupine. When is it ever safe to hug a porcupine? I have found this question difficult to answer, let alone act upon.

I'm told by those conversant with porcupine behavior that porcupines are affectionate and rub against people's legs, like cats, and there's no danger of getting stuck with the spines. Really? That's what I'm told; I have no firsthand knowledge or existential experience. But I'm cautiously willing to give students of porcupine behavior the benefit of the doubt.

Porcupine quills or spines, I'm told, usually lie flat against the porcupine's skin. It is only when the porcupine is alarmed, or feels threatened, that its spines stand up. The porcupine cannot, as commonly thought, shoot its spines at objects of its displeasure. Those spines, however, are easily released and, like the barbs on fishhooks, affix themselves to other mammals only when touched by other mammals. This makes stroking or hugging porcupines no small challenge. The challenge is intensified, of course, if the porcupine's quills are standing up, issuing a strong warning: *Approach with caution! Touch at your own risk!* There is the possibility that the risk might be mitigated if one can get the porcupine's quills to resume their calm posture and lie flat against the porcupine's skin.

This is akin to the pastor's challenge to deal with difficult people, i.e., getting their quills to lie down. Every congregation has in its membership at least one porcupine: a person full of sharp, pointed quills of negativism, habitual skepticism, and persistent defiance of authority.

What causes difficult people's quills to stand up? Allow me to offer one possible answer: unhealed, damaged emotions resulting from past hurts, disappointments, and unfulfilled dreams. Rather, than yield to the temptation to avoid difficult people, pastoral ministry requires that we engage such persons in conversations aimed at helping them find healing for their damaged emotions.

It might be helpful to understand "porcupines" by better understanding ourselves. One or more of the following questions may be helpful for better understanding:

- As you think about your past, what experiences have given meaning to your life? What's the most significant experience you've had during the last two or three years?

- What have been some of your greatest joys? In what ways have these joyful experiences influenced your life?

- What have been some of your greatest disappointments? In what ways have you dealt with these disappointments? What are some of the things you've done to manage these disappointments?

- As you think about your future, what two or three things do you want to see happen in your life? What challenges do you see in your future and what are some of your greatest fears?

In conversing with "porcupines" (difficult people or people who throw stones), the wise and compassionate pastor will listen attentively, without bias, and without body gestures that signal disapproval or approval. Engage in the kind of listening that evidences interest. Offer verbal responses conveying the feeling that what is shared is safe with you. Attentive listening coupled with prayer will encourage difficult people's quills to lie down, thus bringing them closer to finding healing for their damaged emotions.

4. I would do what is necessary to teach congregants how to treat the pastor and his or her spouse and children.

Congregation members, even good-hearted lay leaders, do not always know how to treat the pastor and the pastor's family. The pastor's calling is to be a *pastor-teacher* (Eph 4:11). One of the pastor's teaching responsibilities is to teach people how to treat the pastor, the pastor's family, and the support staff. If the pastor does not feel comfortable teaching people how he or she should be treated, then the pastor should at least do what is necessary to have someone else— perhaps another seasoned pastor—do the teaching. Teaching church members how to treat the pastor is a good gift to bequeath to one's successor.

Healthy churches treat their ministerial and support staff in ways that enable the pastor and the staff to serve with joy. Pastoring is a burden, but healthy churches seek to make it a "burdensome joy." It is my observation that short-term pastorates often result when congregants fail to treat the pastor in ways that make pastoring a joyful experience.

The author of the New Testament Book of Hebrews shares my concern: "Have confidence in your leaders and submit to their authority, because they keep watch over you as those who must give an account. Do this so that their work will be a joy, not a burden, for that would be of no benefit to you" (Heb 13:17, NIV). This verse offers an outline for the development of a curriculum designed to teach congregants how to treat the pastor and his or her family. For example, what does "being responsive to one's pastoral leaders" look like? For starters, submit to their authority. Additionally, what things, what practical acts of kindness can congregants offer to make the work of leadership a joy? What are some things congregants do, perhaps unwittingly, that make things a burden for the pastor and the pastor's family?

Again, if the pastor does not feel comfortable teaching people how he or she should be treated, then the pastor should at least do what is necessary to have someone else do the teaching.

5. I would give attention early on in my ministry to the ever-so-silent sin that exists in all congregations: the sin of domestic violence.

My introduction to the presence of domestic violence in my congregation came far too late in my ministry and with great shock and surprise. I have written about my "awakening experience" in the second edition, pages 150–153, of the book *Domestic Violence: What Every Pastor Needs to Know* by Al Miles. With few editorial changes, what follows is the testimonial confession I wrote.

Awareness that my ministry needed to have more than a passing concern and knowledge about domestic violence came following a Bible study I conducted at my church. Near the end of our study, just before I was ready to dismiss the class, one woman raised her hand and asked, "Pastor, where in the Bible does it say that a wife must obey her husband?"

My immediate unspoken response was, "What does this question have to do with the content of our Bible study?" After glancing at my watch in an effort to send the message via my body language that it was time to go home, I responded, "You raise a good question. Why don't you and I talk about that after our dismissal and closing prayer?" The woman agreed.

Our brief conversation revealed that this Christian woman was currently a victim of domestic violence and had been for years. I was blown away, and in some ways caught void of the necessary pastoral skills and contacts to give her the immediate help she so desperately needed.

Across the next few days, I also learned that others in the congregation had for quite some time already known about her situation. How could I, her pastor, have been so blind? Were there signs and indicators of her suffering that I missed? Yes, I knew that her husband was autocratic and domineering. But I never related this to his treatment of her. After all, they were prominent members in the congregation. They always sat together during worship. Publicly, they spoke well of each other. She was deeply involved in the church and extremely active in the social services of the larger community. On several occasions they had hosted me in their home. From my vantage point, their public lives did not evidence the pain and agony revealed to me during our after-Bible-study conversation.

Because of this experience, I began to give greater attention to the sin called domestic violence. As providence would have it, during this timeframe my church's state organization sponsored a three-day retreat on domestic violence awareness.

By the end of the retreat, my cup overflowed with information I wished I had during the earlier years of my ministry. I found some comfort, however, in the thought that it is always better to learn late than to never learn.

I invited the facilitator of the retreat, himself an ordained Christian minister, to speak on domestic violence awareness during my congregation's Sunday morning service. There were about 175 to 200 worshipers present. What a joy and challenge it was for me to learn even more about domestic violence, and this time with my congregation. Little did I know that I was in for another awakening.

Following the worship service, several women of the congregation confided to me that they were either currently or had been involved in situations of domestic violence. An even greater number asked me to pray for a friend or relative who was currently a victim of abuse. Others thanked me profusely for giving the Sunday morning sermon slot to the critical issue of domestic violence.

Following these experiences, I invited several pastors and community leaders to work with me to plan and conduct a weekend conference on domestic violence awareness. It was well attended.

While there is still more for me to learn about domestic violence, I am grateful to be able to say that my increased awareness and growing sensitivity to this sin has altered the way I go about my priestly duties as a minister. I am now more sensitive to how I handle the Scriptures that are oftentimes interpreted in ways that tend to sanction male dominance and female submission.

Furthermore, I now take advantage of every opportunity afforded me to show compassion for those embroiled in abusive situations. For example, when appropriate, I include in my prayers and preaching comments and information that evidence concern and support for victims of domestic violence. When offering the pastoral prayer, a simple petition asking God to give wisdom, protection, and guidance to those suffering from domestic abuse goes a long way toward sending the message that this pastor and congregation are concerned and ready to help.

I also pray for perpetrators of domestic violence. I ask God to help them to see that, through intensive and long-term counsel, they can over time be helped to live free of the need to dominate and control the individuals they have committed to love. Such prayers and public displays of concern send the message that the faith community is aware of situations of domestic violence and that it is okay, right, and necessary to talk about these issues. It also sends the message that help is available, if not through the faith community then through social service agencies and counselors to whom the faith community can make referrals.

Finally, I have also learned that far too many of my ministerial colleagues are ill-prepared to minister effectively to victims and perpetrators of domestic violence. Although I am not yet where I should be in this area of ministry, I thank God that I am not where I once was.

While I recognize that "with much wisdom comes much sorrow; the more knowledge, the more grief" (Eccl 1:18, NIV), I also recognize that our ministerial calling requires that we bear the sorrow and find ways to manage the grief in the interest of bringing good news to victims and perpetrators of domestic violence.

If I could start my pastoral ministry all over again, I would give greater attention to the sin of domestic violence. I would encourage every pastor—indeed, I urge every pastor—to become conversant with those organizations in the community that specialize in assisting the victims and perpetrators of domestic violence.

Conclusion

Had I been more sensitive to the aforementioned areas of concern early on during my pastoral ministry, my ministry may have proved to be more of a blessing to those whom I was committed to serve. I'm encouraged to know that God gives all of us opportunities to learn and to grow.

About the Author

Robert O. Dulin, Jr., served for thirty-five years as pastor of the Metropolitan Church of God in Detroit, Michigan. During his tenure he demonstrated a strong commitment to family life, community development, and partnering with others to meet the financial needs of community development.

A graduate of Anderson University (BA) and of Central Baptist Theological Seminary (MDiv), Dulin was also the recipient of an honorary degree (DD) from Anderson University. After retirement from pastoral ministry, he served as regional pastor for the Churches of God in Southeastern Michigan and an on-call funeral home chaplain.

Prior to coming to Detroit in February of 1974, Dulin spent five years as the national director of family life and adult education for the Church of God (Anderson, Indiana). In addition to his devotion to his family, he was committed to work and fellowship with all persons of good will, and to helping others achieve their highest potential.

PART III:

A Pastor's Influence upon a Congregation

10. Preaching Wisdom from James Earl Massey

by Curtiss Paul DeYoung

When Dr. James Earl Massey died in June 2018, he had been preaching for over seventy years. I knew Dr. Massey for over forty years. I was first inspired by his preaching when he was my campus pastor at Anderson College (now University). As an undergraduate, I learned biblical interpretation and the importance of worship in his classroom, which are foundations for preaching. As a graduate student at the Anderson School of Theology, I enrolled in two of his preaching courses. When I transferred to the Howard University School of Divinity, I discovered that my preaching professor Evans Crawford was a dear friend and great admirer of Massey. When I took an intensive seminar in preaching from James Forbes, then the noted professor of preaching at Union Theological Seminary in New York, we talked about the influence of Massey on the field of preaching. Through the years, I have heard Massey preach in a variety of settings. In this chapter I want to share some of Massey's wisdom for preachers today.

Preaching Defined

For James Earl Massey, preaching was "a happening in which nature and grace make claim upon each other to effect an end through speech that neither rhetorical nor sociological theory can fully explain."[1] There is always a mystical quality to the preaching moment where God's word inhabits a human voice to speak to a listener's spirit. The act of preaching defies a precise definition due to its divine quality. Massey noted that this human interaction with the divine also makes preaching "a burdensome joy." He explained, "It is 'burdensome' because of the way the preaching and delivery aspects of the pulpit task weigh upon the preacher's selfhood—and with so many unique demands. But preaching is also a 'joy' because of the divine purpose that makes it necessary and the redeeming eventfulness that it can effect for those who receive it."[2] The preparation to preach is done with a weightiness incumbent on the awareness of the sacredness of the moment. The burden and the joy are both appropriate responses to the mystery of preaching.

The Preacher

Preaching is made unique by the vessel from which it emerges. Our life journey informs our preaching. Massey's setting and circumstances shaped his preaching. He heard God's call to preach at age sixteen while preparing for a career as a classical pianist. His musical gifts informed his calling to preach and instructed his mastery of preaching. Massey stated, "I have found so much that has been of transfer value from my years as a music student. For one thing, there is the ability to focus attention on a given text, and to search its structure and the flow of meaning it seeks to give. In addition, the discipline of memorizing has benefited from a background in music. I used to practice at the piano from five to seven hours a day; I had learned how to 'stay put' at the instrument until the score was not only in my mind but in my fingers as well."[3] Massey turned his great discipline for practice at the piano and the memorization of musical scores toward the task of preaching. He learned to stay put in the Bible until his text was not only in his mind but also expressed itself in his manuscript. His music training served his preaching prowess through the years by alerting him to the importance of a disciplined approach and a structured regimen.

Another factor that shaped Massey's preaching was his upbringing in a bicultural setting. He spoke of his early years, "Our family life was influenced by two churches, both from the same denominational background and doctrinal emphases. The one congregation met just four blocks from our house, while the other was located in downtown Detroit."[4] Massey's grandparents were leaders in the downtown Detroit church, which was predominantly black in membership. The congregation that met in Massey's neighborhood was interracial. This bicultural congregational experience prepared him "to understand the meaning and application of the unity theme that was so often treated from the pulpit," and he also "knew the impacting quality of black spiritual vitality."[5] Our childhood experiences and life journey must be fully embraced and deeply interrogated for impact on our preaching. The preacher is a product of her or his setting and circumstances. This background should be enlisted and put to use as we compose sermons.

The preacher must also fully inhabit her or his own personality and temperament. Trying to copy some other preacher will cause one's preaching to lack the feel of the genuine product. Massey saw evidence of these qualities of integrity and integration in the preaching of the late theologian Howard Thurman. "Very early in his ministry Howard Thurman decided that he would present himself and deliver his message in a way that would match subject matter and personality, that he would give himself so fully to the purpose and issue of pulpit work that he would be at one with it all."[6] Thurman recognized this in himself and described his understanding of the sermon as an expression of the preacher's soul.

Yet as important as it is for the preacher to harness her or his own gifts, skills, upbringing, and spirit, God's anointing is what transforms the spoken word into a sermon. The preacher must never promote herself or himself through the pulpit. Massey observed this posture in one of the master preachers of his era, the late Gardner Taylor—pastor emeritus of the Concord Baptist Church in Brooklyn, New York. He commented to Taylor, "Your sermons have never seemed to be self-regarding; when you preach, nothing ever seems to say, 'Well, here I am!' Avoiding selfish ambition and calculated maneuvers, you have remained faithful in the service of the gospel. While the individual quality of your gifts has been nurtured with care, you have had the wisdom to look beyond those gifts for God's enabling."[7] Taylor got out of the way. No matter how gifted we are as communicators, preaching is not about us. Preaching is meant to reveal the majesty and mystery of the God we serve.

God's anointing is the most important part of what makes us preachers. Massey summarized his view of the preacher as a charismatic or anointed agent of the gospel when he wrote, "Charismatic agents have always been able to stand on their own, use their own gifts, assert themselves with high warrant in a cause greater than their own lives. Willing to risk themselves under the influence of a great meaning, they become creative persons of social importance and characters of spiritual persuasion. They become integrative figures, leaders around whom men rally. Although a strong self-image and the ability to project oneself can be natural factors in the lives of some persons, charisma performs its indispensable ministry and accredits their identity in a still higher manner. Those who live unto God, fully committed, experience this, and those whom they serve can bear witness to it."[8] As preachers we must hunger and pray for God's anointing.

Wisdom from Mentor Preachers and Master Preachers

James Earl Massey recommended that one develop mentoring relationships with seasoned preachers and also study what he called master preachers. It is vital for us to find living mentors and models from whom we can gain wisdom for preaching and critique if needed. Massey noted four role models or mentors for his own preaching. The first was his father, George Wilson Massey, Sr. From his father he gained an appreciation for deep learning of the Scriptures. The second was Raymond S. Jackson, the pastor of his youth and young adult years. From Jackson he observed courage in preaching. The third mentor was Howard Thurman. Massey noted, "From Thurman I gained insight into the importance of depth for pulpit work, especially spiritual depth as a witness for God." The fourth model was George Arthur Buttrick, who exhibited "skills in sermon development and…provocative handling of a text."[9] The fourth mentor Massey mentioned,

George Buttrick, was one of the most noted white preachers of his era. Massey's bicultural upbringing influenced not only his preaching and understanding of his listening audience, it even prompted him to seek mentors from outside his church tradition. As the audiences we preach to increase in diversity, it is wise for us to find mentors and models from various cultures, races, and ages, and both genders.

Massey also recommended the study of master preachers. He described these preachers as follows: "The great preachers, the masters of the craft, are those who lay stress upon the dignity of preaching and show that dignity through the drama of their own work in the pulpit. The master preachers are those who honor the preaching tradition from the centuries behind them and cast the vote of their own lives to shape a tradition that will follow them. The master preachers are those who, though not setting out in egotism to become acclaimed a master, nevertheless in humility and honest toil achieve that end."[10] The study of master preachers occurs through listening to these preachers in person, through live streaming, or via recordings. It also happens through careful study of their published manuscripts. According to Massey, there are three ways such study helps:

1. Great sermons reflect a preacher's concern for his or her task and times and the preacher's understanding and concern for the gathered congregation, the realities of their lives, and the spirit of their times.

2. Great sermons reveal how the preacher's personality influenced the preaching style.

3. Great sermons allow us to trace how the preacher related words to the Word. Great preachers are usually word artists, using the language of the people with greater skill than most.[11]

When living mentors are not readily available, one can access a long history of master preachers for study—including Jesus himself, the first master preacher.

Wisdom from the Black Preaching Tradition

James Earl Massey always included an emphasis on the black preaching tradition in his books and preaching courses, yet he was also well versed in the ways of preaching in white communities. His ultimate goal was to inspire bicultural preachers. Massey wanted to develop preachers "equally at home in any pulpit...because within their pulpit work they wedded the best from more than one preaching tradition." He wanted preachers to not be bound by "the ideals of the majority culture and its settings," yet also able to consider dominant culture perspectives.[12]

Massey believed there were "significant insights to be derived from the black preaching tradition, insights which help any preacher from any tradition to sense more clearly how to keep the verbal witness of the pulpit both virile, engaging, and effective."[13] In his teaching and writing, he focused on five aspects of the black preaching tradition: sermons in black churches as functional, festive, communal, radical, and climactic.[14] What follows are some of James Earl Massey's wisdom on each of these aspects.

1. *Functional.* "The sermon is never regarded as a product for its own sake, or even as an art form, but as a means to an end.... The end is to initiate some person into the faith, instruct some person on how to live, inspire some person to go on living with hope despite troubles and strain, give insight into problems and possibilities within and beyond those problems. The sermon is functional in its intent to liberate the hearer's spirit, give life, and sustain faith."[15]

2. *Festive.* "Black preaching is never abstract and tangential. It deals with concrete life, with what is experienced in the daily round, and it does so without arid speculation or poised sophistry. The black sermon is usually 'playful' in its measured cadences and speech liberties. The speech-result is no less true, no less sensible, even when done with 'instinct' and fervid imagination.... Black preaching excels in being an invitation to joy, even in the midst of sorrow and struggle. It does so by means of strong affirmation about God and through the contagious note of witnessed faith. Whatever festivity and playfulness fill the black sermon are there because they have been *won* in the midst of sorrow and lament, making the sermon itself an open expression of faith that has worked its way through, and now speaks in praise of God."[16]

3. *Communal.* "The sermon must aid the sense of group life. The well-known tradition of call-and-response should be understood in this light. Many churches of varying denominational contexts are accustomed to plan a call-response action through a reading, litany, or chant; the black sermon is itself a call for response. The black preacher usually allows for and expects acts of communalism among his hearers, even vocal expressions of praise, agreement, encouragement, and prompting. The speaker's word alerts, calls, promises, energizes, bestows, blesses, challenges, corrects, confutes, chastises, claims, convicts, convinces. Although specific responses among black church audiences will vary in keeping with many factors..., it is not infrequent that audible expressions of response will occur in most black settings where the preacher speaks with festive bearing, for a functional purpose, and with a sense of community with his hearers."[17]

4. *Radical.* The sermon "must take the hearer to the roots of personal life and vital response. More often than not, this radicality demands that the preacher be a person of courage.... Radicality in the sermon engages the hearer. It

makes him know that he is being confronted, that necessity is being laid upon him to respond. True preaching is always confrontational.... Preaching is a special process with a special goal and end in view. Radical means are essential to that process and end."[18]

5. *Climactic.* Black preaching produces *"a climax of impression for the hearer.* The sermon is a functional instrument, based upon a distinctive scriptural word, calculated in faith to win and nurture the life of the hearer. A kind of feeling-attitude is important for a proper response. Zestful speech encourages this result. The will for community, and means for nurturing it, is also essential. So are mind-engaging lines. Imagination also renders its service and continues at that service even while the process of delivery continues.... Preaching is as much contagion as it is conversing; perhaps it is really more contagion than conversing.... A preacher must not ignore the soundness of the theory that his sermon should produce a climax of impression for his hearers."[19]

As I read again Massey's words on the black preaching tradition, I reflect on my own journey as a preacher. I was born and raised in white settings. Yet in my twenties, as I entered the formative years of my preaching calling, I sat under the tutelage of professors of preaching from the black preaching tradition (James Earl Massey, Evans Crawford, and James Forbes); I listened to sermons by master preachers from the black preaching tradition (Gardner Taylor, Caesar Clark, Manuel Scott Sr., Vashti McKenzie, Samuel Hines, Martin Luther King Jr., Cheryl Sanders, and others); and I preached in black congregations in New York City and Washington, D.C. whose members helped shape my preaching through call and response. This multicultural investment has made me the preacher I am today.

Composing Sermons

James Earl Massey felt that preachers should compose sermons that sing! Such sermons take form because of three essentials: "a talent to create," "a controlling sense of order," and "an honest concern for people."[20] Massey emphasized the creative aspect: "It takes talent to create a sermon, a talent whose capacities are stimulated by an encounter with some truth, experience, some aspect of life, but usually an encounter with a biblical text. Engaged attentiveness to a text is essential to creating a sermon because empowerment to preach is linked with engagement with the truth spoken within the text."[21] The preacher must identify what is needed for creativity. For Massey, his background in music inspired his understanding of creativity. Therefore, sermons must sing. For us it might be walking in nature, sitting by a beach, reading poetry, or even observing the hustle and bustle of a busy urban intersection.

The Preacher as Event Maker

Ultimately for James Earl Massey, the preacher needs to become an event maker: "The *eventful* [person] in history is any [person] whose actions influenced subsequent developments along a quite different course than would have been followed if their actions had not been taken. The event-making [person] is an eventful [person] whose actions are the consequences of outstanding capabilities of intelligence, will, and character rather than of accidents of position."[22] Casting the preacher as an event-making person elevates the role and the importance of gospel proclamation. As preachers, we speak words that disrupt and change the lives of people, communities, and nations. Massey summed up his thinking on this point, "Eventful preaching demands an interpreter who is ordered and controlled by the living message in the text. We are sent to share something more than a mere stream of words, however interesting, entertaining, or sensational they might be. We are sent to speak for God and to do so with pointed application for a particular time and people."[23]

Conclusion

James Earl Massey understood preaching as a word that emerges at the intersection of the human voice and the divine intent. Preachers embrace their natural gifts and learn from their life journey, while depending on God's anointing. Massey encouraged us to strive to excel at our craft through encounters with mentors and master preachers, and the study of various preaching traditions—in particular, the black church preaching tradition. Then our sermons will sing and signal life-changing events. In preparation for that moment our preaching days will end, Massey said, "We come into this world and live for a time. We find our work after a time and do our work for a time. Then, in spite of the importance of that work and the successes or disappointments related to it all, we must in time leave it all. That is a reality. And that reality underscores the ultimate importance of The Story entrusted to our telling, for The Story promises and points to the reality of a life beyond this one, and to rewards for faith and faithfulness during our life here."[24] Amen!

About the Author

Rev. Dr. Curtiss Paul DeYoung is the CEO of the Minnesota Council of Churches, which represents twenty-five Protestant communions with a programmatic emphasis that includes racial justice, interfaith relations, and refugee services. Previously he was the executive director of the historic racial justice organization Community Renewal Society in Chicago and the inaugural professor of reconciliation studies at Bethel University in St. Paul.

An ordained minister in the Church of God (Anderson, Indiana), DeYoung has served on staff at congregations in Minneapolis, New York City, Michigan, and Washington, D.C. He is the author and editor of twelve books on reconciliation, social justice activism, multiracial congregations, racism, and the cultural diversity of the Bible. He consults and speaks in the United States and internationally, with extensive relationships among activists and peacemakers in South Africa and the Holy Land.

Curtiss DeYoung has been married to Karen since 1984 and has three adult children living in Chicago, New York City, and Seattle.

1. James Earl Massey, *The Sermon in Perspective: A Study of Communication and Charisma* (Grand Rapids: Baker Book House and The Warner Press, 1976), 104.

2. James Earl Massey, *The Burdensome Joy of Preaching* (Nashville: Abingdon Press, 1998), 13.

3. James Earl Massey, *Views from the Mountain: Select Writings of James Earl Massey*, Barry L. Callen and Curtiss Paul DeYoung, eds. (Glendora, CA: Aldersgate Press, 2018), 241.

4. Ibid., 243.

5. Ibid.

6. James Earl Massey, "Thurman's Preaching: Substance and Style," in Henry J. Young, ed., *God and Human Freedom: A Festschrift in Honor of Howard Thurman* (Richmond, IN: Friends United Press, 1983), 110.

7. James Earl Massey, "Tribute to a Titan," in Timothy George, James Earl Massey, and Robert Smith, Jr., eds., *Our Sufficiency Is of God: Essays on Preaching in Honor of Gardner C. Taylor* (Macon, GA: Mercer University Press, 2010), 3.

8. Massey, *The Sermon in Perspective*, 108–109.

9. Massey, *Views from the Mountain*, 242.

10. James Earl Massey, *The Responsible Pulpit* (Anderson, IN: Warner Press, 1974), 115.

11. James Earl Massey, *Designing the Sermon: Order and Movement in Preaching* (Nashville: Abingdon Press, 1980), 85–86.

12. Massey, *Views from the Mountain*, 255.

13. Ibid., 50.

14. Ibid., 50–57.

15. Ibid., 50–51.

16. Ibid., 51.

17. Ibid., 52.

18. Ibid., 53–55.

19. Ibid., 55–57.

20. Massey, "Composing Sermons that Sing!" 11–22.

21. Ibid., 12.

22. Sidney Hook, *The Hero in History* (New York: John Day Co., 1943), 154, as quoted in Massey, *The Burdensome Joy of Preaching*, 69.

23. Massey, *The Burdensome Joy of Preaching*, 76.

24. Massey, *Stewards of the Story*, 50.

11. Developing a Mission-Minded Congregation

by Robert Culp

Newspaper columnist David Brooks wrote that any side involved in a war needs training in how to wage it, strategies for winning it, and a call to arms that explains why they are in it. No matter the field of endeavor under consideration, this three-part plan has the potential to turn any person or group into a winner. No matter how much energy and good intentions we may have, it can all come to naught without a good plan.

Years ago when I was in college, a group of us, full of zeal, decided we could and should reach out to the community across town with the message of Christ. We pooled our meager monies, put our heads and hearts together, prayed, and planned a neighborhood outreach. A flyer was designed and distributed, music and speakers arranged, and a large neighborhood facility secured and prepared. The night of the event came, and with great anticipation we piled into several vehicles and drove to our destination to await the arrival of the crowd of local people. Not one single guest came.

The expected disappointment following such a fiasco was ours, but we were wise enough to know there must have been a reason for this outcome.

Zeal alone is never enough. Doing some things right is valuable, but it will not bring success. Even when you have done most things well, a successful outcome can still be in jeopardy. There are some absolutes that must always be included.

There is no more powerful teacher in life than experience. The pain that comes from our failures can either cause us to quit or to grow. Failure does not always mean you should simply avoid repeating past unsuccessful actions, pray for better results, or make a few adjustments. It may require the creation of a totally new plan. And no matter how carefully that new plan is put together, further corrections and eventually a whole new strategy may be necessary.

The one common factor among all fields of endeavor is the necessity of change. A lack of change, or resistance to it, has ruined people's best-laid plans. If we are closed to change, what worked yesterday may fall flat tomorrow. Everybody from Baby Boomers to Generation Z resists change to some degree—especially Boomers, whose love of power and authority make change a constant threat. So included in every plan there has to be a subplan whereby a strategy for implementing the new plan can be made effective.

To sum up what we are aiming at in this writing, there must be more than one strategy, more than words on a page, and more than good intentions if we are to develop a mission-minded congregation. There must be the three things David Brooks wrote about: a call to arms, an effective strategy, and sufficient training to win this war we are engaged in.

A Call to Arms That Motivates

There are periods in the life of a nation or a people when it seems that nothing changes. There are other times when it seems the world is changing so rapidly that it is difficult, if not impossible, to keep up. It is not easy and sometimes even feels unnatural for the church to fulfill its mission in the world.

In the church we have to successfully accomplish our mission or we will go out of business. Each year churches are closing not by the hundreds but by the thousands. It would be easy to simply decide to hang in there and make survival our goal, but thank God there is a better way. If we can "light a fire" under our people, the world will come to experience the light and warmth.

Let's be honest. Church services can be boring, but the right sermon kindles a spiritual spark that calls for further exploration. This kind of sermon comes from a minister who has been stirred. It will lead to motivated saints "catching" what is happening to their leader. God's plan for motivation, then, works for the leader but also includes the follower. The leader must put together a biblically sound and psychologically motivating plan that will move the needle of spiritual enthusiasm in the congregation.

Choosing a slogan for the plan that is catchy and motivating is important. I once preached a sermon with the title "Changing the Atmosphere." For some reason that only God knows, it "exploded" among my people. I heard that phrase repeated every day for weeks, and it eventually became the next year's theme for our congregation. A concept that I initially feared would be a bit too heavy or too deep for the average believer caught fire and produced wonderful results.

At First Church of God Toledo, we focus on a new theme every year. The theme not only provides a catchy slogan to motivate the membership, but it reminds us of how we are to fulfill our vision and mission as a church. "Changing the Atmosphere" challenged us to remember our mission statement: Our mission is to be a loving family of praying Christians who celebrate in worship together, witness everywhere to reconcile persons to Christ, disciple every convert to spiritual maturity, and become trained and involved in ministry to one another and the world to the glory of God. We seek to make sure the "atmosphere" or culture of our church is conducive to the fulfillment of this mission.

An Effective Strategy That Works

Strategies are fairly easy to come by. Churches typically just do a little adapting to what have become traditional or common practices, and this may work—for a season. But long-term success requires much more.

Generational changes are being recognized and documented more and better than ever. The characteristics that dominate each particular generation are well established. Strategies for reaching and affecting these generations have to be arrived at carefully, skillfully, and prayerfully. One thing that can help to unite generations is the realization that we are here to change the world—and changing the world, its culture, and its people will take the best effort we can put forth. An effective strategy is not an option but a necessity.

Strategies: Something to Have and to Hold

The New Testament church, as described in the Book of Acts, illustrates how the apostle Paul effectively communicated the gospel in a variety of ways to a variety of cultures. Recently, while purchasing a pair of socks, I noticed a sign on the rack that also seemed to express the sentiments of many churches. It said, "One size fits all." To think that we can use this approach in leading the body of Christ is wishful and disastrous thinking.

The strategic approach to ministry has finally come of age to many church leaders. There is a growing cluster of strategies that are proving to be effective in the twenty-first century, but no one strategy works everywhere for everybody. An effective church can be a megachurch, but it can also be a house church. Doing something different just for difference's sake is not satisfactory, either.

In developing a strategy for the church, a prayer emphasis is essential to discern the mind of God. Effective decision-makers in the life of the church will spend much time in prayer. It is a ministry that is essential for any growing congregation.

The Right Strategies: Large and Small

A leader ought to spare nothing in reviewing the structures, strategies, and activities that comprise the local church's approach to serving people. Congregations have traditionally structured their ministries to serve specific age groups, from the nursery to the seniors and everything in between. A certain "sacredness" grows up around these ministries. It's almost as if there is a sign, unwritten but still very obvious, that says, "Do Not Disturb." In some places, to even consider abolishing the men's ministry, the women's ministry, the couples' club, or the singles ministry would seem tantamount to eliminating the church's value and purpose altogether.

Even if the plan ends up leading to the elimination of some programs, this should never be its focus. The goal is not to simply eliminate but to create ministries that best serve this day and time. Change just for change's sake is not only boring, it could be disastrous.

Putting phrases such as "changing the culture" or "reaching our neighborhood" into action in the congregation requires the right strategy. The basic energies and resources of many churches serve a strategy that is traditionally directed to a different purpose. Is it too demanding to start over, at least in our thinking?

The Right Strategy: Go Make Disciples

According to the New Testament record, Jesus was quite plainspoken in his instructions to his followers. Matthew 28:19 (NIV) records it this way: "Go and make disciples of all nations." If disciple-making is to be the single most important priority of the church, our present structure and functioning seems to have gone astray at some point. Our typical ministries and meetings are centered on a "come" mentality rather than an emphasis on "go." For many years we have formed a church culture that is centered on people coming to services at the church building.

Another factor that has kept us from fulfilling the Great Commission is the necessary work of caring for our sheep. This task has become so significant that it has successfully overpowered all impulses to prioritize our mission to the world. Our facilities serve as a helping and healing station for the saints, and our organizations serve to benefit the appetites of God's people.

Sometimes it seems that the mission of the church is to sustain itself. Still, the words of Christ keep echoing in our minds: "Go and make disciples." To do this effectively, we have to do some serious shifting of priorities and structure. One of these moves is from being so program-oriented and centering on self-promotion.

The Strategy for Transitioning

Transitioning to an effective plan for the church of today has its obstacles and drawbacks. Older generations, who embrace yesterday's values and priorities, should not be left out. A simple solution is that we start with a transitional plan, taking advantage of the limited resources we have and being sure yesterday's efforts and people are not forgotten.

The deacon board or other leaders of the church should be as active as ever. It is no small task to minister to the sick and those who are homebound. Writing notes of encouragement and making phone calls are simple but significant actions. The inclusion of former leaders makes sure they are not forgotten, and their wisdom can help avoid the pitfalls of change.

When reorganizing the church structure, we cannot outrun the need to change the values of the flock. You cannot and should not change one without the other. Leaders must be informed and informing. Meetings should carefully enlighten people so they are aware of societal and religious trends. Church folk need to understand that denominational distinctions are no longer on the decision-making list of church-seekers. The interest in worship is still high or maybe even higher. Teams are important, and consensus is more important than a majority vote. Most of all, relevancy is demanded.

At First Church of God Toledo, we know that, in order to make disciples, we must first reach those who do not know Christ. To reach unbelievers, we must go into our community, not only taking the gospel but also becoming salt and light, meeting the needs of those we come into contact with. The church must leave the building. Over the years we have developed a strong presence in Toldeo. Our vision statement describes our task to "reach non-Christians of all ages through creative ministries that address urban needs." Examples of how we have sought to accomplish this include:

- First Church of God Day Care and Christian School
- FACTS/FORWARD Program for persons addicted to drugs and alcohol
- Sparrows Nest Women's Shelter for homeless women
- Family House Shelter for homeless families
- Four Corners Afterschool Program and Summer Day Camp providing tutoring and character building for students K–12
- Food at First Afterschool Program providing meals for students and families
- School supply and uniform giveaway

In addition to the local community, we have been involved nationally and globally, planting churches in several states and supporting foreign missions through the ministry of the Boudreauxs in Haiti for many years.

Training That Assures Success

Christ was the champion disciple-maker, and his followers changed the world. The apostle Paul built on this and likewise was wonderfully successful. We may not do it exactly as they did, but with this basic model we can achieve a significant level of success. Jesus' companions were called disciples; Timothy was Paul's apprentice.

Whatever the terms used, a model of mentorship has been set for us. It involves not simply the passing on of information but the establishing of a vital relationship. As we mentor others in the church, one vital element that makes the relationship productive is a commitment to "missional intentionality"—training others to understand and embrace the congregation's mission.

How can you implement training that assures success at developing a mission-minded church? First of all, come up with an overall statement such as a congregational vision statement that spells out what your church's primary reason for existence is. This statement should be an expression of what you believe God's purpose is for your congregation.

Try to refrain from a generic, all-serving statement that could be used by any church. Your vision statement should be specific to the call of *your* church, providing the foundation piece that the rest of your actions are built on.

Second, every mission-minded church needs a strong spiritual foundation. With this in place, we can think outside the box as never before. Innovative worship will help greatly, for the day is over for doing the usual "routine" stuff.

Third, effective ministry in the twenty-first century requires a recognition of lifestyles that are very different from those of yesteryear. Once upon a time, people came to church. Now, we must take the church to the people. No longer do we need to just sit back and envy technology's impact on people's lives; we must embrace it as a tool for effective ministry. E-church, texting, live streaming, and many other innovative ways of communicating the gospel can become effective avenues into the lives of people.

In response to sociological changes that have impacted the "church gathered," First Church of God Toledo has increased its social media presence. In addition to streaming our worship services, we also provide Bible studies using video conferencing as well as conference calls. Corporate prayer is conducted through these platforms as well. This allows us to not only stay connected with our membership but to connect with non-Christians and with believers in other geographic locations. On any day of the week, our groups will consist of people locally as well as from across the country.

Fourth, small groups are coming back. Ministry through small groups in the church can make the building of trust simpler and more effective. It also allows the leader to listen and know people's stories better. In small groups, you can share the mission and vision of the church in more personal and relative ways. Small groups provide multiple times and means for customizing the gospel story to the needs and interests of different people.

Conclusion

The goal of the local church should be greater than the growth of the local church. Christ died for the whole world, and the aim of every local assembly should be to make the good news available to all people. Short-term missions to other parts of the country and world should be included in every overall plan. But even our jobs, our neighborhoods, our hobbies, our families, our friendship circles, our local fitness centers—these places all afford the opportunity for trained believers to share a powerful witness for our Lord.

About the Author

Bishop Robert A. Culp has been senior minister of First Church of God in Toledo, Ohio, since 1961. He previously served at the Williams Street Church of God in Danville, Illinois, and has been involved with founding and planting congregations in Little Rock, Arkansas; Jackson, Mississippi; Lima, Ohio; and Toronto, Ontario, Canada. He and his wife, Maggie, have four grown children and four grandchildren.

Culp holds a Bachelor of Arts degree from Anderson University in Anderson, Indiana, and a Master of Divinity and honorary doctorate from the Anderson University School of Theology. He has been chairman of the General Assembly of the Church of God, president of the National Association of the Church of God, and president of the National Inspirational Youth Convention, and has served on the Ministries Council of the Church of God, the Anderson University board of trustees, the Board of Christian Education of the Church of God, and the board of Christians Broadcasting Hope (CBH).

12. The Pastor as Key Steward
by Rudolph Smith

This chapter seeks to call attention to the importance of stewardship in the life of the church and particularly in the lives of pastors. It is the culmination of my long-time interest in the subject of stewardship that grows from activities in many different settings: sermons delivered, classes taught, seminars and workshops conducted on various occasions, times of study, and personal insights. As a pastor for many years, I realize the vital role that pastors play in promoting sound stewardship in their congregations.

In reviewing the concept of stewardship in the New Testament, there are a couple of words in the Greek language that speak persuasively to pastors as the primary stewards of their congregations, adding perspective to the broad range of responsibilities of the pastoral role:

- *epitrepo* means to administer someone's goods. Paul saw himself as an administrator or steward of the mysteries of God: "This, then, is how you ought to regard us: as servants of Christ and as those entrusted with the mysteries God has revealed. Now it is required that those who have been given a trust must prove faithful" (1 Cor 4:1–2, NIV).

- *oikonomeo* means to steward or manage. Luke 16:1–15 tells of a shrewd manager who was required to give an account of his stewardship.

The New Testament usage of *oikonomos* is descriptive of the duties and responsibilities of a manager, a trustee, or an administrator. The *oikonomos* was one who was not the owner but who was delegated to oversee or manage the property or affairs of the owner. From the parables of Jesus, we gain valuable insight into the nature of our stewardship.

A steward is always a servant. Often the two words are used interchangeably. The steward is a servant who may be placed over other servants. In the passage from Luke 16, the steward or manager is one who has been entrusted with his master's affairs. What has been placed in his care does not belong to him, yet he has been charged with the task of safekeeping the owner's goods and properties. The parable stresses the steward's accountability for not handling properly and securely what had been entrusted to his care. From the parable we learn that good stewardship means preserving and keeping safely that which has been entrusted to our care.

The New Testament Greek word *epitrophos* refers to one who is a manager, a guardian, or a foreman. Stewardship involves being a trustee, a caretaker. A steward is one to whom something has been entrusted for safekeeping or proper use. The owner does not want any diminished returns on his investments.

As one who has been given oversight or management over someone else's property, possessions, or affairs, the steward must handle this assignment responsibly. The parable spoken by Jesus in Luke 12:42–48 offers valuable insight into the nature of our stewardship. In this parable, the steward or manager is one who must responsibly fulfill the master's assignment.

Our spiritual growth and development are either promoted by our recognition and practice of certain stewardship principles or impeded by our failure to do so. We must acknowledge God's sovereign ownership as Creator of all that exists, our own dependency as finite creatures, and our ultimate accountability to the Creator for our stewardship of the life he has given us. Our stewardship is the consequence of God's ownership as the Creator of all things.

The Basis of Ministerial Stewardship

Pastors are responsible to act as proper stewards in the context of ministry. Our stewardship as pastors is the outgrowth of God's ownership of all that was created. The basis of our stewardship lies in the fact of God's sovereign ownership as Creator. Despite the various theories of the origin of the universe, we maintain that there is intelligent design behind its origin. The Scriptures offer a simple, plausible explanation: "In the beginning God created the heavens and the earth" (Gen 1:1, NIV). This is a statement of faith declaring that God is the Creator of this universe and all that it encompasses. While God remains an ultimate mystery, we can know him through his self-revelation in the Bible and particularly through Jesus Christ.

The Breadth of Our Stewardship

In considering the breadth of our stewardship, we raise several questions. What are the scope, the extent, and the boundaries of our stewardship? As stewards, what is entrusted to our care? What has been given or bestowed upon us to manage responsibly before God? Is stewardship really a crucial life issue?

We affirm again that stewardship involves the whole of life, that no arena of life is exempt from stewardship implications and applications. Life itself is a gift from God; it is God's breath pulsating in us and sustaining us. This truth is the basis of the conviction that stewardship involves the totality of life.

The Parable of the Bags of Gold given by Jesus in the Gospel of Matthew provides instructive insight into the scope and nature of our stewardship: "It will be like a man going on a journey, who called his servants and entrusted his wealth to them. To one he gave five bags of gold, to another two bags, and to another one bag, each according to his ability" (Matt 25:14–15, NIV).

The Stewardship of Talents and Giftedness

The Master calls us his servants and distributes resources to each of us *according to our individual abilities*. This part of the Matthew 25 parable reveals a vital aspect of our stewardship, the stewardship of talents and giftedness. While the resources mentioned in this parable have to do with money, Jesus' teaching has greater significance if we apply its contemporary meaning for didactic purposes. If the resources God gives us are understood as natural or specially acquired abilities, or natural or physical aptitude, or abilities of a superior quality, then the parable has great relevance for us. With this perspective in view, let us now consider the stewardship of talents or giftedness, the abilities we each possess, and how these relate to the idea that stewardship involves more than money.

In Matthew 25, what each servant received was "according to his ability" (v 14). It is a fact of life that we humans are not all equally gifted, that we differ in our natural endowments mentally and physically. God has bestowed upon each of us talents and abilities that differ. While we are not responsible for the endowments given us, we are responsible for the development and use of them. How then do we differ, and what accounts for the difference in our giftedness? Paul's words to the church in Rome are insightful: "I urge you, brothers and sisters, in view of God's mercy, to offer your bodies as a living sacrifice, holy and pleasing to God—this is your true and proper worship" (Rom 12:1, NIV). Whatever we have, we are to give it all to God in service.

The Stewardship of Freedom

Stewardship involves the freedom of choice, as we see in Deuteronomy 30:19 (NIV), "This day I call the heavens and the earth as witnesses against you that I have set before you life and death, blessings and curses. Now choose life, so that you and your children may live," and Galatians 5:13 (NIV), "You, my brothers and sisters, were called to be free. But do not use your freedom to indulge the flesh; rather, serve one another humbly in love." In the Parable of the Bags of Gold in Matthew 25, the master left and "went on his journey" (v 15) after disbursing the bags of gold. In his absence, the servants were left on their own, each free to decide what he would do with the money entrusted to his care.

Each servant in the parable could do something or nothing, be industrious or idle, work or loaf; each could invest or not invest, take risks or play it safe. We too have been endowed with freedom to choose since God has given us free will in this life. Will is the arena of choice. Choice in life confronts us daily. There are major choices and minor ones, some very important and some less important. Choice is woven into the very fabric of life; it is an inseparable consequence of our freedom of will. Thus, freedom to choose is an integral aspect of our stewardship.

The mind—the ability to think—is one area in which God gifts us; it is where we make choices. In his Letter to the Ephesians, Paul prayed for these believers that God "may strengthen you with power through his Spirit in your inner being" (Eph 3:16, NIV). Note that the "inner being" is to be strengthened or empowered by the Holy Spirit. What did Paul mean by the "inner being"? The inner being is the reason, the conscience, the will. These terms all describe the function of the mind.

An important work of the Holy Spirit within us is to clarify our thinking, to sensitize the conscience and energize the will by the renewing of the mind (Rom 12:2; Eph 4:23). Our minds are renewed as we internalize the Word of God: "I have hidden your word in my heart that I might not sin against you" (Ps 119:11, NIV). A mind that is saturated with the Word of God is enabled to think clearly and soberly as we develop godly character.

Character is a factor in the choices we make, as it impacts our conscience. Conscience is crucial because it is the arena of moral choices. The conscience is where our moral values and our sense of right and wrong live; it is the seat of our ethical and moral sensitivities. The conscience is developed through training, teaching, and instruction. No child is born with a ready-made conscience. Conscience is educated; it is the result of our upbringing, of the moral and ethical values instilled in us—or the lack thereof.

The admonition to "start children off on the way they should go" (Prov 22:6, NIV) is wise counsel for every parent. The Scriptures speak about the development of a "good conscience" (Acts 23:1; 1 Tim 1:5) and a "clear conscience" (1 Tim 3:9), and they warn against having a "seared conscience" (1 Tim 4:2), a "weak conscience" (1 Cor 8:7), or a "guilty conscience" (Heb 10:22).

Marriage is a choice we make in this life; it is possible to be married but also to be single, and there is nothing wrong with either state. Our eternal destiny is also a choice we make—a vital one. To spend eternity in the presence of God or be banished forever from his presence is a decision each person must make personally.

Choice is inevitable in life. Everybody must choose and does choose, multiple times a day, day after day. And everybody has to live with the consequences of their choices, whether good or bad. Like those servants from Matthew 25, we too are free to choose what we will do with the resources entrusted to us. We therefore conclude that the stewardship of freedom is an inescapable reality of life.

The Stewardship of Instruction

The stewardship of instruction or learning is another important area for pastors and ministers of the gospel to consider and understand. In the Parable of the Ten Minas in Luke 19, the master gave these instructions to his servants: "Put this money to work…until I come back" (Luke 19:13b, NIV). These words introduce the element of instruction as an integral aspect of our stewardship. Stewardship involves the instruction from God as to how we are to live during our earthly sojourn.

The instructions for how we put our resources from God to work for him are found in the Bible. It is our textbook for matriculating successfully in the school of life. Its precepts are to prepare us for eternity. Since God as Creator has the right of ownership to determine how we should live, he has rightly given instruction in his Word to guide us in every area of life. God has a purpose for each of us in this life, and our gifts and talents enable us to fulfill that purpose.

The Scriptures contain far too many directions and admonitions to be included in these pages. We endeavor, however, to keep a few important ones in mind, among them the Ten Commandments given by Moses (Ex 20:1–17). It is noteworthy that Jesus condensed all of God's commands into two basic principles: to love God supremely and to love others as we love ourselves (Matt 22:34–40).

The Stewardship of Time

In regards to how we spend our moments and our days, the apostle Paul admonished us, "Be very careful, then, how you live—not as unwise but as wise, making the most of every opportunity, because the days are evil" (Eph 5:15–16, NIV). How we use our time is another crucial component of our stewardship before God. Each of us has been given an allotment of time, which we may use wisely or wastefully. Time can never be recovered or reclaimed, therefore how we use our time, whether wisely or foolishly, affects the caliber of our stewardship.

We are all given time to develop and use our God-given talents and abilities to honor the Lord and be a blessing to others. Devoting our time to God through godly pursuits such as worship, prayer, Bible reading, and meditation is a proven key to a productive and fruitful life. The parables of Jesus suggest that our stewardship of time here has implications for our eternal reward hereafter. Specifically, we conclude that time spent serving God in this life results in spending eternity in his presence, while those who do not serve and honor him will spend eternity banished from his presence (Matt 25:31–46).

The Stewardship of Opportunities

Life confronts us with many opportunities. In the Parable of the Bags of Gold from Matthew 25, the three servants faced the choice of doing something or nothing with what was given them. Two were willing to take risks; the other was not. Life often confronts us with challenges, with risk-taking choices, in which we must exercise faith in God and in ourselves in order to achieve personal goals as well as God's will for us. Do we pass up opportunities for a better education, jobs, and other challenges that often seem insurmountable? Quite often God will place us in circumstances of uncertainty in order to test our faith and our commitment to him. The servant with the one bag of gold failed because he had no faith in himself nor his master. Deciding to play it safe, he buried his money in the ground and lost his reward. It is axiomatic that God supremely tests those whom he highly rewards.

The Stewardship of Possessions

It hardly needs to be argued that stewardship of possessions is a fact of life. The fact that we brought nothing into this world and will surely carry nothing out (1 Tim 6:7) is proof positive. No matter how much wealth and other possessions we accumulate, there comes a time when we will leave it all behind. The crucial question for each of us is, *What do I do with my possessions?*

Whatever we possess or think we own is held temporarily at best. A basic tenet of our faith is that we are only stewards or caretakers of whatever God allows us to possess in this world and that we must give account of our stewardship in the life to come. As servants to whom the Master has entrusted his property, we will acknowledge his right of total ownership and give accountability for our stewardship when he returns. May we ever be mindful that only faithful stewards are rewarded.

There can be no denying that we have a stewardship of the influence we possess. All of us have influence upon others as a result of our relationships. Some common relationships include parents and children, neighbor and neighbor, teacher and students, employer and employee, friends and friends, and many others that could be listed. Our influence may be good or bad, positive or negative. We would do well to remember the words of our Lord, "Let your light shine before others, that they may see your good deeds and glorify your Father in heaven" (Matt 5:16, NIV).

The quality of our life, character, and deeds should make them beacon-lights of positive influence upon others that bring honor to God. We are challenged to be faithful, influential stewards. Our stewardship of influence is closely related to and greatly dependent upon our stewardship of example. As Christians, we should be good role models for others, whether in the home, the church, the school, the workplace, or the community. Our attitudes, spirit, lifestyle, etc. should be exemplary and contagious.

The apostle Paul urged his young protégé Timothy to "set an example for the believers in speech, in conduct, in love, in faith and in purity" (1 Tim 4:12, NIV). This counsel to model stewardship by precept and example is also for us today. It has been said that it is always better to *see* a sermon than to hear one. Each day we leave footprints in the sands of time that impact others.

Conclusion

The writer of Ecclesiastes, after attempting and evaluating all the pursuits we might possibly seek in life, offered this counsel of our accountability: "Now all has been heard; here is the conclusion of the matter: Fear God and keep his commandments, for this is the duty of all mankind. For God will bring every deed into judgment, including every hidden thing, whether it is good or evil" (Eccl 12:13–14, NIV). As pastors and ministers, may God find us to be good and faithful stewards in our management of the talents and giftedness, the freedom, the instruction, the time, the opportunities, and the possessions he has given us.

About the Author

Rev. Dr. Rudolph Smith, a retired pastor who established the Community Church of God in Atlanta, Georgia, in 1966, is a revered teacher, preacher, and theologian, a magna cum laude graduate (MDiv) of the Interdenominational Theological Center (ITC), and recipient of the Doctor of Divinity degree from Warner Southern College (now Warner University) and the Doctor of Humane Letters degree from Anderson University. He has over sixty years of experience in ministry, traveling extensively across the United States and around the world.

Dr. Smith has served as the dean-director of the In-Service Training Institute (twenty years), an associate campaign fund director (twenty-five years), and the national budget chair (ten years) for the Church of God (Anderson, Indiana), and was the first recipient of the ITC Richardson Ecumenical Fellowship Distinguished Alumni of the Year award. Smith is the author of *Stewardship: More Than Money*, a book offering a holistic view of stewardship that encompasses the totality of life. He and his wife, Edna, reside in Atlanta, Georgia.

13. Church Administration

by Maxwell Ware

How is it that a bumblebee can fly? It has wings that are too small, and its body and head are too large. It appears that it is not really designed to fly. However, anyone can go into a garden and see a bumblebee going about its business. It is as though God is demonstrating that even such a creature of nature must depend on something supernatural to sustain it. The bumblebee never questions its ability to fly; it just goes ahead and does its job.

Like the bumblebee, we must understand that regardless of how hard we try it is totally up to God to sustain us in our Christian flight. This chapter pertains to how we cooperate with God in the area of church administration and organization. As pastors and ministers we must still flap our wings as we partner with God in the work of his kingdom.

Some may think the area of church administration is to be viewed through a secular set of filters. I believe, however, that church administration is as spiritual as any other area of ministry in the church. We should approach it from a spiritual perspective and seek God's guidance as we do in all other areas of ministry.

The acrostic FORWARD covers the following broad areas and provides a pathway to move forward in the area of church administration and organization:

- **Facts** and **faith** must be blended together.
- **Organize** to accomplish your objectives.
- **Restore** with God's purpose in mind.
- **Work** for Christ and with one another.
- **Administer** with God's help.
- **Remember** God's promises and **rejoice** in them.
- **Discern** the challenges of the future.

Facts and Faith

Facts and faith work hand in hand. The first thing to do in solving any problem is to understand all the facts pertaining to the situation. Know your facts! We should not be afraid of the facts.

Before we can do anything in establishing goals, we need to know and understand the facts before us. What are the risks? This should be determined before we proceed with any course of action. Before you make any decision, an assessment should be made of the direction you want to travel.

The Book of Nehemiah gives us an excellent model of a committed, God-honoring leader. Nehemiah inspected the walls of Jerusalem at night, so he would understand the extent of the work that needed to be done before he presented the proposed work to the people. Once we know the details of the situation before us, we will be in a better position to begin the work.

There is an assessment that each pastor must make of his or her flock. What is the condition of the people financially? Do you have consistent givers? Are they tithers? Are they on fixed incomes? Are they professionals who have ample salaries? You must know that you have people who will consistently give before you take on any financial project. You must first assess all risks before you make the appropriate decision.

There are many young ministers who begin to pastor before they know the condition of the flock. Their expectations of future increases in salary and benefits are not shared by the leadership of the congregation. Your expectations should be realistic and not based on speculation about the future.

Can you live on the income that is being provided at the current time? If you are willing to take the present salary with the expectation of future benefits as the church grows, this should be outlined in an employment agreement. I believe every pastor should have a written agreement so that it is clear to everyone what has been agreed upon.

Over time, the people who serve on and lead church boards change, so the pastor's salary and any benefits should be documented. Financial pressure on a leader in ministry is like financial pressure on a marriage, which can lead to frustration, disenchantment, and poor decisions.

Clear financial expectations and procedures also benefit the congregation. As pastor and shepherd, you must protect your people. Although you may have integrity and would never fleece the sheep, there may come a pastor after you who does not have your kind of integrity of heart.

Make sure your congregation is protected with appropriate bylaws. I would recommend that the church's bylaws be reviewed by an attorney who is familiar with nonprofits and churches. The bylaws should address how to resolve church conflict and give instructions for disposition of property in the case of the dissolution of the church, among other things.

I believe that a church should be pastor-led rather than board-led. In today's culture of democratic rule, many members try to bring that style of leadership to the church. Certainly a pastor is foolish if he or she does not speak with other church leaders before making a decision. But the final decision should rest with the pastor, in consultation with the elders of the church and other key leaders.

Organize

Once you have assessed the situation, determining the associated facts and approaching things in faith, it is time to develop a plan to accomplish the work. We must get organized! When Moses' father-in-law Jethro observed Moses judging all the people by himself from morning till night, he asked Moses, "What is this you are doing for the people? Why do you alone sit as judge, while all these people stand around you from morning till evening?" (Ex 18:14, NIV). Moses then divided and delegated leadership. Many pastors try to do too much by themselves. We must learn to delegate.

The story of Nehemiah tells us that he divided the work on the wall in an organized way. And not only was Nehemiah a brilliant planner, organizer, and motivator, he was a man of prayer. Every plan should be saturated with prayer. I am a firm believer that prayer is critical to any planning. Proverbs 16:3 (NIV) states, "Commit to the LORD whatever you do, and he will establish your plans." Rather than taking my own plans to the Lord, I would rather have a plan dropped into my heart *by* the Lord. This is the difference between a good idea and a God idea.

Nehemiah constantly prayed and trusted God, while making plans at the same time. He organized the people to do the work, assigning certain tasks to certain families. He lived in a tribal society, so he used those natural divisions to divide the work. Delegation is often hard for pastors in small churches, because they think it is easier to do all the work themselves. A pastor may feel that taking the time to explain things to others and train them to do the work will cause a loss of momentum.

As the church grows, the need for organizational order and direction grows as well. A formal leadership structure should be outlined in your church bylaws—one that includes groups to provide counsel to the pastor without usurping the pastor's leadership. The church is not a democracy; it is a theocracy. I have made it a practice in my church that all major decisions and policies are reviewed in joint consultation before being implemented. There is no voting, but we try to reach a consensus on all issues. The group of leaders weighs in on decisions regarding policies, vision, and our financial responsibilities. In addition, the pastoral staff is consulted for most major decisions.

Restore

God is in the business of restoration, and he will go with those who are seeking to do his will and win others to Christ. Our objective is to keep our eyes on the goal, which is to help people find the Lord Jesus Christ and experience a new, abundant life in him.

The story of Nehemiah tells us that he worked in Susa as a personal assistant for the king of the vast Medo-Persian Empire. Nehemiah was concerned about Jerusalem because it was his people's holy city. He sought information about the status of the Jews remaining there. He prayed and asked God's guidance. After getting permission from the king, he traveled back to Jerusalem. His heart was broken when he found that the city wall was broken down and its gates had been burned with fire. Nehemiah developed a plan for restoration and presented the plan to the leaders in Jerusalem, who responded, "Let us start rebuilding" (Neh 2:18, NIV). The people rallied around the call and began the process of restoration.

God has called us to do his work. He touches people's hearts when they see the need.

Jesus Christ is the only way into God's kingdom, but different churches and different techniques are able to attract different people. Many congregations are still "fishing" with the same bait they used when they first started out, but are now not catching much of anything. Remember, we should be married to the message and not the method.

I believe that one must be called to be a pastor. It is not a job or a career that you decide on pursuing. God must put within you a pastor's heart to care for the people who are placed under your care.

God called David the shepherd boy to be king over Israel. Psalm 78:70–72 (NIV) says, "He chose David his servant and took him from the sheep pens; from tending the sheep he brought him to be the shepherd of his people Jacob, of Israel his inheritance. And David shepherded them with integrity of heart; with skillful hands he led them." In church administration, there must be integrity and leadership skill. David's good heart made him a good shepherd, and he guided the people wisely and well.

In John 21, Jesus asked Peter three times, "Do you love me?" and told him, "Feed my sheep." God is concerned about his sheep and places shepherds over them to care for the sheep. Sadly, so many people are "fleecing the sheep" today, taking advantage of them rather than feeding them or helping them be restored to a relationship with God.

Work

One must put in the work in order to receive the reward. God is not going to bless you unless you do the work. The wall around a city was important in ancient Israel because it was a primary means of protecting the city. Nehemiah arrived quietly at Jerusalem and spent several days observing. He got firsthand information and carefully considered the situation. After he had assessed the condition of the wall and determined the facts, he then presented the work for the people to perform. He kept his mission secret until he was ready to go public.

Timing is critical in getting agreement from people for doing God's work. Sometimes we present our ideas prematurely before we have a chance to fully develop them, and they get shot down before they can get off the ground. *You must know who the influencers are in the congregation and get their buy-in.* Moreover, people must see clearly the work that needs to be done. A good leader must bring it into focus.

Nehemiah saw the situation. It was God who put the desire in his heart to help. Then God put the plan in his mind for how to approach the work. Nehemiah presented a realistic strategy to the people—a realistic one that he had carefully designed. He presented his plan with confidence and enthusiastically shared his vision. We must be careful not to underestimate people; sometimes they only need to see the vision clearly and be challenged with it.

Let us keep in mind that words have power; when we share the vision, we are filling the air with words of faith. When Nehemiah presented his plan to the people, they caught the vision and their response was to start the work of rebuilding.

Whenever you have a good plan, opposition will come. Nehemiah 4:1–2 (NIV) states, "When Sanballat heard that we were rebuilding the wall, he became angry and greatly incensed. He ridiculed the Jews, and in the presence of his associates and the army of Samaria, he said 'What are those feeble Jews doing? Will they restore their wall? Will they offer sacrifices? Will they finish in a day? Can they bring the stones back to life from those heaps of rubble—burned as they are?' " Sanballat and others criticized the work Nehemiah and the people were doing. Nehemiah and the Israelites overcame this opposition through reorganizing; Nehemiah revised the plan.

How do you respond to criticism? Criticism can be an indication you are on the right track. Don't stop the work! The purpose of the opposition is to hinder, to slow down or stop the progress. The enemy's objective is always to get you embroiled in controversy. When faced with opposition, don't stop. Just keep on preaching, teaching, administering, and organizing through faith and God's Word. If it is beyond your control, let it go!

Administer

Once the church is working toward a goal, you must continue to lead, helping the people continue to visualize the goal and never losing sight of the objective. This takes the work and the gift of administration.

The story of Jesus walking on the water is a good illustration of what Peter was able to do when he kept his eyes on the Lord. When Peter got out of the boat and walked on the water himself, he was okay as long as he kept his eyes on Jesus. But when he took his eyes off Jesus, he began to sink. In the church we can get distracted from our objective because of the strong winds and waves that begin to come our way. One wave may be that of success. If you get puffed up, you can easily fail. A wave of self-importance can easily bring you down.

Another "wave" or distraction can be that of opposition to the work. Success will bring opposition. You cannot focus on the distraction; as a wise leader, you must keep your eyes on the goal of completing the task at hand. Nehemiah had gotten word of Sanballat and Tobiah's opposition to the work. They began to ridicule and threaten the workers and the wall.

Some people are fine with the way things are; they do not grasp the vision of what is being accomplished. Because Sanballat and Tobiah were not part of the work, they criticized it. They were satisfied to live with the disgrace of the city wall being in shambles. Nehemiah, however, was motivated, and he continued to anticipate success. His goal was to complete the rebuilding of the wall. He never lost track of that objective, but he had to make an adjustment to his plan.

When it appeared that an attack was immanent, he made an adjustment to the organizational structure. He devised a plan of defense that would unite and protect his people—half the men were to work, and half were to stand guard. We should be also be willing to adjust when something is not working.

If you are overwhelmed by an assignment, remind yourself of God's special purpose for your project or church. More importantly, remember that you are doing this work for God. And finally, remind yourself and others that you are not in the battle alone. If the enemy comes to attack you, remember that our God will fight for you.

One thing I have learned is that you cannot do everything yourself. Pastors must learn to administrate by delegating. Many leaders take on projects themselves rather than making their team members accountable. Don't carry the crosses of others—let them carry their own.

Remember and Rejoice

Continue to remember God's promises. If God promised it, he will do it! The good work that he has started in you, he will see to completion (Phil 1:6). Don't get tired of the good work you are doing, for the harvest is coming! When you are doing a work for God, you can expect to receive God's help. He will always do what he said he would do. When the task is finished and we cross the finish line, we must remember all that God has done and rejoice in it.

Nehemiah and the workers celebrated the completion of the wall. We should also stop to celebrate how God has brought us through. We should realize and give thanks that it was only through God's grace that we were able to achieve the victory. As the old saints used to say, "I look back and wonder how I got over!"

When Joshua crossed over the Jordan, God instructed him to have twelve men from each tribe memorialize this great miracle of God cutting off the waters and bringing them through the river on dry land. Revelation 12:11 (NIV) states, "They triumphed...by the blood of the Lamb and by the word of their testimony." It is important to speak up and share the good things we remember.

Psalm 119:11 (NIV) says, "I have hidden your word in my heart that I might not sin against you." It is remembering God's Word that keeps us from sinning. Hiding the Word in our hearts is a deterrent to sin. This alone should inspire us to memorize scripture. God's Word makes us wise. The Bible is completely true and trustworthy. True wisdom goes beyond amassing knowledge; it is applying that knowledge in a life-changing way. The Word sanctifies, and it is dependable for guidance and help. Let us remember what God has said and done and rejoice in it.

Discern

The Bible teaches us to watch as well as pray. When things are going well in the church, it is no time to rest on our laurels—we must continue to be on our guard, always casting vision to enable us to stay focused on our assignment. We need to discern any future challenges that may crop up to stop the work.

After the Israelites had rebuilt the wall, Nehemiah returned to his responsibilities with King Artaxerxes. He later came back to Jerusalem and found that one of the main opponents to rebuilding the wall, Tobiah, had been given his own room in the temple. And the people had begun to fall back into their old covenant-breaking habits. They had promised not to allow their children to intermarry with foreign nations, but during Nehemiah's absence they broke their vow to God. Nehemiah was filled with righteous anger. He kicked Tobiah out of the temple and made the people renew their vows not to intermarry with heathen nations.

In the church, we must resist going back to the old way of doing things, which typically means our way. Sometimes the "Tobiahs" of our old life want to take control. When this occurs, we must purify the temple and kick the enemy out. With our people, we must renew our commitment to embracing the vision and accomplishing God's work.

I believe discernment of the future is a matter of perspective and our positional authority in Christ. Our churches must succeed because Christ is with us. How do we see ourselves? Are we looking through the eyes of faith? Or are we looking at the problem? Through what lens are we viewing things? A measure of faith is required in church administration. In fact, there is a supernatural gift God provides in this area—just as much as he provides gifts of healing and miracles. You should not look for just good businesspeople to serve as leaders in the church but people of wisdom and faith who can help you discern future challenges the congregation may face.

Conclusion

Nehemiah knew that he would be successful in his work because "the gracious hand" of the Lord was upon him (Neh 2:18, NIV). There is a great song by Preashea Hilliard that states, "I am expecting great things." Let us develop the perspective that great things are on the way! We are reigning in this life with Christ. May we choose to believe that great things are on the way. Let us humbly and boldly move forward as administrators of God's church.

About the Author

Maxwell H. Ware has been the senior pastor of Cornerstone Church of God in Columbia, Maryland, for over twenty years. Pastor Ware grew up in Columbus, Ohio, and served in various lay-capacities prior to being called to ministry in 1969. He received an MBA from Adelphi University in Garden City, New York, and a bachelor's degree from the University of Nebraska in Omaha, and has also studied at Central Bible College (now part of Evangel University) in Springfield, Missouri.

Ware has served on the Warner Press board of directors and is presently chairman of the elder board of the Chesapeake, Delaware, and Potomac District of the Church of God. Before entering full-time ministry, he was employed by several Fortune 500 companies and held a number of middle management positions. He is also retired as a major in the United States Army.

Rev. Ware's wife Beverly passed away in 2010. In that union he was blessed with five children and seven grandchildren. In 2014 he married Sheila Baratta Ware, who now assists him in ministry.

14. Effective Leadership

by Edward L. Foggs

The terms "leader" and "leadership" are used in a variety of ways in our society. Very often these words are referenced as a matter of title such as the president or the chair or "the boss" or the person in charge, or by rank such as the number one or number two person in terms of position or authority or influence. Leadership in the Christian context, however, transcends these human designations and descriptions.

Jesus' disciples, at one stage of their journey, thought of leadership as "being the greatest." They contended among themselves as to which of them would be the greatest leader—the number one disciple of Jesus. Jesus responded to their competitive spirit with these words of rebuke: "You know that the rulers of the Gentiles lord it over them, and their high officials exercise authority over them. Not so with you. Instead, whoever wants to become great among you must be your servant...just as the Son of Man did not come to be served, but to serve" (Matt 20:25–28, NIV). In this passage, Jesus did not condemn "greatness"; instead, he lifted up a higher measure or standard of greatness.

It is not wrong for leaders to be great, but their greatness needs to be a byproduct of their servant spirit and style. I remember reading a statement one time that said if servanthood is beneath you, then leadership is beyond you.

Leadership is too frequently ascribed to title or position rather than to servanthood. Granted that the person who holds key positions or offices ought to be a leader, but that is not always the case. The president, the board chair, the chief trustee, or some other office holder may come to that post as an authentic leader *or* just as an astute politician, clever enough to manipulate others to achieve his or her private desires, goals, and objectives.

Leadership is included in the biblical list of spiritual gifts. In Romans 12:6–8 (NIV), Paul wrote this about spiritual gifts: "We have different gifts, according to the grace given to each of us. If your gift is prophesying, then prophesy in accordance with your faith; if it is serving, then serve; if it is teaching, then teach; if it is to encourage, then give encouragement; if it is giving, then give generously; *if it is to lead, do it diligently*; if it is to show mercy, do it cheerfully" (emphasis added). Those who have the responsibility of leadership should take it seriously.

It seems appropriate to pose the question, "How then should a leader lead?" Volumes have been written on the subject, but I would venture to voice some of my observations and perspectives in the spirit of the New Testament writer Luke, who began his Gospel with these words: "Many have undertaken to draw up an account of the things that have been fulfilled among us.... I too decided to write an orderly account for you" (Luke 1:1, 3, NIV).

I have pondered more than a dozen qualities that should be evident in the life of a leader. My list is not exhaustive, but illustrative. I will highlight a select few of them.

Leading with Integrity

We live in a society where integrity seems far removed from the values of many persons who serve in leadership roles. Sadly, the lack of integrity can even ooze into the lives of church leaders. This is by no means a blanket indictment. It does, however, reflect one of the realities evidenced in our times.

I have taken the liberty to insert the word *integrity* in the first three verses of 1 Corinthians 13 (NIV) for emphasis, fully recognizing that the apostle Paul was writing about the virtue of love. I think I do no violence to the biblical impact of this passage when I insert this word with reference to leaders: "If I speak in the tongues of men or of angels, but do not have [integrity], I am only a resounding gong or a clanging cymbal. If I have the gift of prophecy and can fathom all mysteries and all knowledge, and if I have a faith that can move mountains, but do not have [integrity], I am nothing. If I give all I possess to the poor and give over my body to hardship that I may boast, but do not have [integrity], I gain nothing." The absence or loss of a leader's integrity weakens and blemishes one's influence, one's achievements, and one's legacy.

Leading with integrity suggests leading by *example*. There is an old saying that goes, "Don't do as I do; do as I *say* to do." That's quite unlike Paul's admonition to the young minister Timothy to "set an example for the believers in speech, in conduct, in love, in faith and in purity" (1 Tim 4:12, NIV).

Another way to think of leading by example is to *model*. One endeavors to demonstrate, illustrate, and show the way in the spirit of Jesus Christ. The failure to lead by example is, in effect, the essence of hypocrisy—feigning to be what one is not, saying one thing and doing another. It is behavior that contradicts what one claims to believe.

Leading with Wisdom

When Solomon came into his leadership role as king of Israel, he recognized his need for wisdom. Hear his prayer: "Now, LORD my God, you have made your servant king in place of my father David. But I am only a little child and do not know how to carry out my duties. Your servant is here among the people you have chosen, a great people, too numerous to count or number. So give your servant a discerning heart to govern your people and to distinguish between right and wrong. For who is able to govern this great people of yours?" (1 Kings 3:7–9, NIV). God was pleased that Solomon asked for wisdom, and he replied, "Since you have asked for this and not for long life or wealth for yourself, nor have asked for the death of your enemies but for discernment in administering justice, I will do what you have asked. I will give you a wise and discerning heart.... Moreover, I will give you what you have not asked for—both wealth and honor" (1 Kings 3:11–13, NIV).

Solomon recognized his limitations. Even though he succeeded his father as king, he realized that good leadership skills are not inherited. Of all the blessings and benefits he might have prayed for, he chose to pray for wisdom.

No leader, no matter how gifted, is so well equipped that he or she does not need divine wisdom. Mere human wisdom has its limitations. It sometimes is biased, short sighted, flawed, or just honestly mistaken. Divine wisdom gives insight, perspective, understanding, and clear focus.

Leading with Vision

It is possible for a person to have 20/20 vision with human eyes and yet possess little perceptive or spirit-led vision. On the other hand, it is possible for a person to be deprived of natural sight and yet have keen spiritual vision. I am not suggesting that these are mutually exclusive. Rather, I am making a distinction between ordinary human vision and the kind of vision leaders need to possess. For it is possible to *look and not see* beyond mere surface realities.

The famous Christian songwriter Fanny Crosby became blind within the first six weeks of her life and was blind for the rest of her life, yet she developed a keen sense and vision of Jesus Christ and the Christian faith. During her lifetime she wrote thousands of Christian hymns, many of which continue to be sung decades after her death. The musical and poetic vision she had has inspired generations of the followers of Jesus Christ as reflected in some of her better-known hymns and spiritual songs, including "All the Way My Savior Leads Me," "Blessed Assurance," "Near the Cross," "To God Be the Glory, "I Am Thine, O Lord," and "Take the World, but Give Me Jesus."

131

Coupled with vision, of course, is the need for *purpose* and *future focus*—vision that probes the question, "For what purpose and to what ends?" Without purposeful and focused vision, there can be no effective leadership. I leave it to the reader to ponder the significance of this idea.

Leading with Conviction and Action

Every leader needs to be a person of conviction. What one believes is pivotal to how one leads. Strong leaders are persons of strong conviction! Strong conviction inspires loyal followers. Strong conviction builds confidence. Strong conviction impels persons to action.

Strong conviction needs to be coupled with timely and meaningful *action*. One of the more common criticisms of leaders is their failure to act. Talk without action often leads to frustration and discouragement. I am reminded of the violinist who spent all of his time tuning his instrument but then never got around to actually playing a tune.

Leading with Compassion

To have compassion means to feel with passion for a person or a cause. It can also mean to enter sympathetically into a person's sorrow or pain. The minister who learns to lead by embracing compassion will have acquired a valuable attribute in his or her arsenal of Christian qualities. In Ephesians 4:32 (NIV), Paul reminded the recipients of his letter (and us), "Be kind and compassionate to one another, forgiving each other, just as in Christ God forgave you." The compassionate Christian leader demonstrates hope, ministers healing, and offers help to those who are suffering spiritually or emotionally.

Conviction is a good thing, but it can be dangerous if it is not coupled with compassion. Conviction can actually be so passionate that it lacks compassion. Conviction can be ruthless, bowling over any and all persons who do not fit into a certain mold.

One thing Jesus repeatedly modeled for us was the spirit of compassion as he ministered to the multitudes. He was without doubt a person of conviction, and he was beyond question a person of action. But it was his compassion that undergirded it all and changed lives.

Leading with Respect and Gratitude

Being a leader can be heady stuff. There can be the temptation to think that the world revolves around *me*—my thoughts, my plans, my aspirations, my preferences, my way. Such an attitude, if not checked, can lead to disrespect for others. In some of my recent devotional reading, I came across this statement: "To belittle [others], you have to be little." No leader has the right to disrespect those who have called him or her to a position of leadership. After all, if there were no one to lead, how could you be a leader?

Respect and gratitude are companion qualities. There is something about human nature that is more responsive when gratitude is expressed. "Please," "Thank you," and "I appreciate it" elicit far more favorable responses than "Because I said so." Every leader ought to be grateful that he or she has been called by God *and* called by the people to serve. To flaunt one's call in the face of those one leads is an act of ingratitude.

Leading with Emotional Maturity

Sometimes a deterrent to respect and gratitude is *emotional immaturity*. Leaders who are emotionally immature often project that same disposition onto those in their circle of influence. Such immaturity can breed tensions and conflict that lead to strife and division. Emotionally immature leaders are emotionally insecure and may be suspicious of others out of their own personal fears and anxieties. Often they are resentful of criticism or ideas that may unsettle their preferred way of doing things.

There is a book I have recommended to many leaders across the years entitled *Overcoming the Dark Side of Leadership: The Paradox of Personal Dysfunction* by Gary L. Mcintosh and Samuel D. Rima, Sr. The authors seek to urge those in leadership to confront the warning signs of potential failure, which they term the "dark side." The "dark side" refers to the inner urges, compulsions, and motivations that drive one toward success. The book helps leaders to understand what the dark side is and how to discover one's own dark side, and it offers guidance on steps to redeem one's dark side. Its insights can be a great tool for moving toward emotional maturity.

Leading as a Continual Learner and Effective Communicator

Learning is a lifelong pursuit. If ever a leader adopts the attitude that his or her formal credentials should be punctuated with a period rather than with a semicolon, such a leader is in for serious trouble and frustration. There is always more to learn by reading, by interacting with professional colleagues, through exposure to new ideas, methods, and procedures, and by venturing beyond "the way we've always done it." One who refuses to be a continual learner may manage to lead a *surviving* operation but not a *thriving* enterprise.

Clear communication is also essential to effective leadership. It is not adequate just to have creative ideas. I suspect that many good ideas have floundered because they were not clearly communicated. If people do not understand what you are proposing, they are not likely to be motivated or inspired to implement the idea or proposal. Communication is not clear unless and until it is understood.

In the very early years of my pastoral ministry, I preached what I thought was a decent sermon. At the close of the service as I was greetings congregants, a young college student said this to me: "Pastor, you told us everything we ought to do, but not a thing about how to do it." Afterward I reviewed my notes—and concluded that the student was right. It is possible for leaders to inspire people to the point of frustration by failing to provide handles that communicate clearly how to pursue and achieve the desired result.

Conclusion

Obviously there is much more that could be said about characteristics and traits essential to effective leadership. While techniques of leadership merit attention, the spirit and quality of leadership determine its lasting impact and legacy. The serious and conscientious leader can find volumes of resources in print or online that address the essentials of effective leadership in church life. It is my hope and prayer that the contents of this brief chapter will whet your appetite to pursue the topic further.

About the Author

Dr. Edward L. Foggs is a native of Kansas City, Kansas. Following high school, he moved to Anderson, Indiana, to attend Anderson College (now University). Foggs responded to God's call to Christian ministry by spending his lifetime serving in a variety of assignments, including pastor, educator, church executive, author, and community/civic leader. He has fulfilled local, national, and international assignments within the Church of God (Anderson) and also through numerous ecumenical relationships. Dr. Foggs has been the recipient of numerous citations and awards in recognition of his leadership influence.

While based in Anderson, Indiana, Foggs served as pastor of Sherman Street Church of God, an adjunct faculty member at Anderson University, director of urban ministries, and general secretary/CEO of the leadership council of the Church of God. His ecumenical assignments have included work with the American Bible Society, the World Relief Corporation, the National Association of Evangelicals, U.S. Church Leaders, the National Conference of Black Churchmen, and the religious advisory committee of the National Urban League.

Dr. Foggs is a champion of strong family life. He and his wife, Joyce Delores (Stone), were blessed with five children and were married for over sixty-five years before her passing in 2020.

PART IV:

A Pastor's Role in Specific Ministries

15. The Pastor and Family Ministry

by Alvin Lewis

Few people would deny the importance of building strong families in our congregations. However, for some reason we are sometimes unable to make the connection between strong families and strong churches. The two are integrally linked together. When our families are strong and healthy, our churches will likewise be strong and healthy. Sound families produce sound congregations.

Here are some realities about the relationship between the church and the family, and rationales for having a strong ministry to families in the local congregation:

1. The church and the family are united in spiritual and interpersonal relationships that require commitments toward growth in understanding, love, and spiritual renewal.

2. The church and the family are highly related in helping to build solid social, political, educational, and religious foundations in the community.

3. The church and the family are involved in societal and institutional changes and must discover solutions to avoid dysfunction and moral decline.

4. The church must strive to help families deal with family conflict, role confusion, and the formation of viable family relationships.

5. The church must evaluate its resources to see how these resources help families in addressing and solving relationship issues.

There are some basic assumptions I wish to make before discussing the specifics of family-life education in a church setting. First of all, it is the biblical mission and mandate of the church to minister to families in creative and dynamic ways. The church is in a unique place and position to minister to families. The church is called to minister by addressing the spiritual, social, emotional, and educational needs of its members. Many churches possess a variety of people, resources, and social networks to help meet the needs of their members, their communities, and those beyond their local boundaries. And finally, in times of family crises, the church and the pastor are sought to bring healing and hope to broken and bewildered families.

Defining and Discovering

Any worthwhile enterprise or undertaking must have a clearly defined purpose for being. Family-life education and ministry in the church is a worthwhile enterprise and begs clear definition. A broad purpose of family-life ministry for local congregations is to minister to individuals and families in various stages of their development. This includes married couples, singles, older adults, children, and youth.

This definition provides a useful foundation, but where do we go from here? How do we discover specific family needs in the church? One of the initial concerns for family-life programming is the "felt" needs of congregational families. Here are some fundamental questions to be asked when doing an assessment of needs:

1. What do persons as individuals in families need in order to function as helpful family members?

2. What do family units—all kinds of families—need to function most effectively as whole families?

3. What forces are affecting families in our church and community? Which of these are destructive and should be opposed or overcome? Which are positive and should be reinforced?

4. What are some of the potentialities of our families' growth and ministry? Which of these possibilities should be stimulated or strengthened?

As families move through different developmental stages, congregational leaders need a way to identify the needs of each phase of family life. A simple family survey form similar to the one that follows can be distributed to the members of the congregation for their feedback. This is just a starting point; you can make additions or adaptations depending on the dynamics of your own church.

General Concern	None	Little	Some	Much
Pre-marital education	____	____	____	____
Couples enrichment	____	____	____	____
Family worship	____	____	____	____
Living the single life	____	____	____	____
Family financial planning	____	____	____	____
Teaching Christian values	____	____	____	____
Sex education for teens	____	____	____	____
Parent education	____	____	____	____
Inter-generational meetings	____	____	____	____

Growing old gracefully	____	____	____	____
Planning for retirement	____	____	____	____
Family Bible study	____	____	____	____
Parent/child communication	____	____	____	____
Coping with death	____	____	____	____

Building a Strategy for Family Ministry

To build an effective ministry to families, you will need to organize persons who carry a burden and have some abilities and skills to get the job done. The selection of an alert and dedicated group of leaders will help get a family ministry program off to a good start. This group could become the nucleus of a family task force or committee. It is also important for a church to move slowly and to plan carefully so a family ministry program does not end in frustration and confusion.

Here are a few suggestions for getting started in the right direction in your congregation:

1. *Develop family awareness and appreciation.* Guide church leadership to evaluate what is already being done in terms of family ministry and what should be started.

2. *Have a personal study on family life.* Whether you are a clergyperson or layperson, you will be able to speak and share from a stronger position of understanding if your reading on family life is current.

3. *Guide church leadership in study.* Ask that church leaders take turns reading a book on marriage and family life and then present a brief review at a board meeting.

4. *Have resources available for the congregation.* Be sure your church library has an ample selection of books, magazines, audio pieces, and other resources on marriage and family life.

5. *Develop an official family ministry task force.* This will be a committee representative of the congregation at large. Such a task force may include current church leaders, but it could also involve several people from the church who have an interest in families and their development. Be sure to invite children and young people to be a part of this task force as well.

6. *Plan informal intergenerational activities.* Offer special events such as intergenerational workshops or fellowship experiences. Summer, for example, is often a time when other activities have shut down for several weeks. This can be an excellent time to offer something new and exciting.

7. *Evaluate results.* Seldom if ever is a program without need for improvement, especially the first time around. Staff meetings, comments from participants, and more formal feedback from questionnaires can be utilized for program revision. Here are some questions to consider when analyzing the information collected on the survey sheets:

- What kinds of people and resources are in the congregation to assist in meeting discovered needs?

- What community agencies are there where experts may be recruited for family workshops?

- How can our church help families address identified issues?

- What are the resources and services to which some families may be referred?

- How may biblical patterns of behavior help family members fulfill God's intent for the family? What are some of the ways the church can empower families to fulfill their biblical mandate?

- What kind of criteria will be established for assigning a priority rating to family needs? For example, needs could be rated on a scale from *1* through *3*, with *1* receiving the highest priority, *2* the next, and *3* the lowest priority.

Family Bible Studies

An essential part of the planning process to meet family needs is to develop a methodology to help the church plan programs that will reach families at various stages of the life cycle. The final part of this chapter is intended to help Christian-education planners achieve this task. As one complements the other, the church's mission of teaching the Bible will become easier and more effective.

Following are four Bible study sessions that have been designed to help families become better acquainted with God's Word. Each of the sessions includes a Bible study component along with some exercises to involve all participants in the group. These sessions are adapted from my book *Strategies for Educating African American Adults* (Chicago: Urban Ministries, Inc., 2006), chapter 10, "Bible Studies for the Family." They are suitable for married couples, adult Sunday school classes, or any other group interested in learning more about marriage and family living from a biblical perspective.

All of the sessions include the following elements:

- Materials Needed
- Reflection Thought
- Goal(s)
- Bible Reading
- Group Discussion
- Closing Discussion

SESSION 1

GOD'S PURPOSE FOR MARRIAGE

Materials Needed

Chalkboard or flip chart, paper, pencils

Reflection Thought

To become one flesh means much more than just a physical union. It means that two persons share everything they have, not only their bodies, not only their material possessions, but also their thinking and their feeling, their suffering, their hopes and their fears, their successes and their failures. To become one flesh means that two persons become completely one in body, soul, and spirit, and yet they remain two different persons.

Goals

1. To explore some biblical concepts and teachings regarding the institution of marriage
2. To share whatever insights that result from the Bible passages the group will examine

Bible Reading

Genesis 1:26–28; 2:18–24; 5:1–2

1 Corinthians 7:2, 28

1 Timothy 5:14

Hebrews 13:4

1 Corinthians 7:39

2 Corinthians 6:14–18

Matthew 19:3–12

Ephesians 5:21–31

Group Discussion

1. Depending on the size of the group, you may wish to divide into smaller groups (four or five people) and assign one or two of the Bible passages to each. Following the reading of these verses, ask each group to come up with a definition of marriage based on the portion of the Bible they read.

2. As leader, direct the group in a discussion of Genesis 2:24:
   - What is implied in the phrase "leaving father and mother"?
   - What is the meaning of "being united" to your spouse?
   - What is meant by "becoming one flesh"?

3. Discuss with the total group their understanding of Genesis 1:26–28 and 5:1–2:
   - Point out to the group how both passages deal with the male and female being created equally.
   - As the leader, you will probably want to do some research on the meaning of the words *Adam*, *man*, and *woman*. Be willing to share with the group whatever insights you have gained from your research.

4. Discuss the following questions with the group:
   - In what ways are men and women the same?
   - In what ways are men and women different?
   - Does the Bible affirm the equality of the sexes, or does it affirm inequality of the sexes? Explain.
   - What qualities do men admire most in women?
   - What qualities do women admire most in men?

Closing Discussion

Ask each person to write on a piece of paper three things they admire in their spouse. Allow couples to exchange their responses with each other and discuss them. How do the things class members admire about themselves compare with the things their spouses admire in them?

SESSION 2

REBELLION, RUIN, AND RECONCILIATION

Materials Needed

Chalkboard or flip chart, paper, pencils

Reflection Thought

One of the characteristics of adolescence is changing family relationships. Many parents and teenagers fear adolescence because they equate changed relationships with alienation. In their view, adolescence is a time to "become your own person" or to "stand on your own two feet." Of course that would mean saying goodbye to closeness and doing things together. Is that right? No! Just because relationships change doesn't mean that they have to get worse. For some families, the teen years are the closest and best.

Goal

To gain biblical insight and understanding about conflicts that arise from family discord

Bible Reading

Genesis 27:11–36; 33:8–11

Luke 15:11–32

Group Discussion

1. Read the above passages, or have someone in the group do the reading. After the passages have been read, share some of the highlights from them. For example:

   • Both Jacob and the prodigal son each operated out of a mode of self-interest.

   • Jacob and the prodigal son caused resentment and grief among family members.

   • Both Jacob and the prodigal son were repentant of their misdeeds.

   • Jacob and the prodigal son each learned some costly lessons from their indiscreet and intemperate behavior.

   Do not attempt, at this stage, to engage in a lengthy exposition on the above points; just briefly introduce them to provoke some discussion in the group.

145

2. Divide your group in half. One group will deal with the passages in Genesis on Esau and Jacob and the other group will deal with the passage on the prodigal son. If the two groups are extremely large, you may want to further divide them into even smaller groups of ten to twelve. (The additional smaller groups will also discuss one or the other of the assigned passages.) Ask the groups to complete the following statements:

- When I think of Jacob/the prodigal son, I think of…
- In this story, I really feel sorry for…
- If I had been Jacob/the prodigal son, I would have…
- If I had been Esau/the elder brother, I would have…
- The following things really speak to me in this story…

As the leader, allow time for the groups to share some of their thoughts and opinions that were generated from this activity within their small group and then with the larger group.

3. Distribute blank sheets of paper to the total group. Ask them to write the names, or some kind of symbols, of three or four persons with whom they have had personal conflict, they have been hurt by, or they have had negative feelings about. Have the group respond to the following questions after they have written down their list of names:

- In what way(s) did this person hurt me?
- For what reason did this person hurt me?
- Did I tell this person I was hurt by his or her words or deeds?
- Did I pray for this person and for myself that our differences would be resolved?
- Have I forgiven this person for hurting me?

Please keep in mind that this is not an easy activity for persons to participate in; therefore, you will not want to coerce those members of the group who feel uncomfortable doing this exercise.

Following this activity, you may wish to allow some persons to talk about the difficulty they had in making up a list and responding to the questions. Ample time should also be allowed for persons to express what they have learned from this experience.

Closing Discussion

Conclude this session by reading the following verses: Ephesians 4:26, 31–32; Matthew 5:23–24; 18:15–17. Offer a closing prayer on behalf of the members of the group or ask several volunteers to offer brief prayers.

SESSION 3

BUILDING SELF-ESTEEM AMONG
FAMILY MEMBERS

Materials Needed

Chalkboard or flip chart, paper, pencils

Reflection Thought

What comes to your mind when you think of the word *esteem*? Consider such ideas as valuing the worth of another person, thinking well of ourselves, or showing respect or appreciation for others.

Goals

1. To develop deeper interpersonal relationships among church and family members

2. To discover insights from the Bible to build esteem in the self and in others

Bible Reading

Ephesians 4:25–32

Philippians 4:8

Colossians 3:8–14

Group Discussion

1. Allow about twenty minutes in small groups of five or six for participants to read and discuss the meanings and spiritual implications of the three Bible passages in reference to building esteem in the church and in the family. Be sure to assign to each group one of the passages. If you have more than three groups, it is okay to assign the same passage more than once.

2. Following the small-group discussions, draw a vertical line down the center of the chalkboard or a flip chart with the word *church* on the left side and *family* on the right side. Ask the groups to share some of their thoughts on building esteem in the church and in the family. Summarize on the chalkboard or flip chart, and discuss ideas further where appropriate.

3. Ask each person to write the names of the members of their families on a sheet of paper. They should then write three things they like about each family member whose name they have written down. Encourage group members to not write anything negative about any family member.

Closing Discussion

Ask group members to rearrange themselves in their original small groups. They should look again at the passages they originally studied, but this time they should work together to come up with a list of "Ten Commandments for Family Relationships." Portions from these lists can be shared with the larger group. You might assign a committee to choose the best of the "Ten Commandments" to present to the entire group at your next meeting.

SESSION 4

FAMILIES THAT PRAY TOGETHER

Materials Needed:

Chalkboard or flip chart, paper, pencils, hymnals

Reflection Thought

Just as oxygen sustains the human body, prayer supports the Christian family. Prayer provides the flow of God's energy that enables families to cope with crisis, live in harmony, comfort those who are restless, and encourage those who are disheartened. Talking to God through the medium of prayer is a step that moves families toward maturity in Christ and love for one another. It has been proven that families who *pray* for one another seldom *prey* upon one another.

Goals

1. To gain an appreciation of the meaning of family prayer
2. To enrich one's personal life through the exercise of prayer

Bible Reading

Exodus 33:12–17

Exodus 10:46–51

2 Chronicles 7:14

Luke 18:1–8

Group Discussion

1. Divide the large group into four smaller groups and assign one of the passages on prayer to each group. Following the reading of the passage, each group should come up with a definition of prayer. Caution the groups to make their definitions complete but not too long. Then ask each group to share its definition with the other groups. In a positive way, point out any similarities or differences among the definitions.

2. Ask the groups to reflect on persons they know who are hurting and in need of prayer. Encourage each group to share one or two names from their list of hurting persons. The groups could take turns praying for one another's

requests. If there are members of the church family who need prayer, be sure to include them also.

3. Ask family members (nuclear or extended) to form small circles and pair off with another family member (e.g., father-daughter, mother-son, brother-sister, uncle-nephew). Have them share personal prayer concerns with each other and then each family member pray for the other.

Closing Discussion

As a final activity, ask the group to list the characteristics of prayer using the first letters of the word *PRAYER* to begin each statement (here are some examples if anyone needs help):

P—power

R—refreshing

A—ask

Y—yield

E—examine

R—renewal

Allow for brief discussion on the words that were generated from the PRAYER acrostic and conclude with the hymn "What a Friend We Have in Jesus."

Conclusion

Effective pastoral leadership means building strong families in the congregations we serve—for the good of the families themselves and for the good of the church. The church has a unique and distinct opportunity to minister to families by the spiritual, social, emotional, and educational needs of its members. As we help our people grow in understanding, love, and spiritual renewal and evaluate the church's resources to see how they can better help families in addressing and solving relationship issues, our congregations will become fountains of healing and hope for individuals and families who desperately need it.

About the Author

Rev. Dr. Alvin Lewis earned his PhD (Adult Education and Adult Development), MS, and BS degrees from Kansas State University in Manhattan, Kansas, and his Master of Divinity degree from Garrett Evangelical Seminary in Evanston, Illinois. Dr. Lewis served as national director of adult and family life education/leadership development for the National Board of Christian Education of the Church of God, Anderson, Indiana, from 1974 to 1989. From 1989 to 1992 he was the executive director of the National Association of the Church of God, West Middlesex, Pennsylvania. From 1992 to 1999 he served as administrator and minister of pastoral care at the Vernon Park Church of God in Chicago, Illinois.

Lewis is the author of *Strategies for Educating African American Adults*; *Older Adult Resource Manual*; and *Directions: A Manual for Local Church Ministries*. He and his wife, Dr. Juanita Lewis, have three children: Alvin Vaughn, Lydia Janese, and Lystrelle Daneen.

16. Ministry to the Sick and Shut-Ins

by Linda L. Braggs

With the leading of the Lord, it was part of my responsibilities at the Emerald Avenue Church of God in Chicago, Illinois, to develop a ministry to the sick and shut-ins of our congregation. The first tool for this ministry was a monthly in-home mini-worship service, which served twenty to thirty persons per week. The pastor of our congregation, along with the leadership board, approved me as coordinator of this program to lead twelve groups of saints in monthly visits, understanding that some were not available for every visit. Most groups would visit two or three persons on the same Sunday. Each group served both members and non-members of the church led by an approved minister, deacon, or lay member of the church. One couple in the church purchased Communion kits for the groups to use in their ministry.

Making the Visit

The coordinator would call each home on the Saturday before to get clearance from the person or the person's caregiver to grant us permission to come on the following day. Volunteers gathered following the worship service for assignments and prayer. The leaders then led small groups of saints to homes, hospitals, and nursing homes, providing a mini-worship service, appropriate literature, Communion to those who were saved, and a recording of the morning worship service when the home was equipped with the appropriate device.

When we returned to the church after ministering, we were served a delicious meal by a volunteer group. We would recap our experience and report obvious needs to be attended to.

Development of a Service Registry

We soon realized that many of those we visited were perhaps not sick but only shut in. They were not able to drive or catch a bus to church; they were not able to comb or cut their hair, prepare their meals, or dress for trips outside the home. They could not cut the grass or clean their homes. Sometimes the caregiver was in great need of a break. Many were alone and at the mercy or whoever would come and provide for them.

153

Seeing this, the coordinator established a service registry for those in need. Members of the church would sign up for the days, times, and services they could provide and the number of hours they could give. General information was passed along to those in need. When they had a need, we provided the service through the coordinator, who maintained the service registry.

Development of Senior Camp

Realizing that the state of a person's mind and spirit affects her or his health, that, as Proverbs 17:22 (NIV) says, "A cheerful heart is good medicine, but a crushed spirit dries up the bones," we saw that the people we were visiting needed some cheer. Providing for their physical needs was good, but they needed more. We wanted to make them kings and queens for a day. We needed to provide a balanced program. We came together and worked out a plan whereby we provided transportation for those who could not provide their own, bringing them to the church for "senior camp" one day per week for four weeks for four hours each time during the month of July. July was significant because the church's teens would be out of school; we could hire them and train them to work for the camp.

We set up a committee to plan a well-rounded fun and educational schedule that included devotional time, singing, games, crafts, lunch, speakers who were spiritual and educational, and fun activities for the mobile and for the not-so-mobile. We recruited volunteers from the congregation who were willing to donate their time for the joy and success of the camp and who loved and understood seniors. The coordinator worked with the volunteers, listened to their ideas, and, whenever possible, developed those ideas into a workable part of the schedule. It is important to include the ideas of others into our programs and ministries when we can; otherwise we cause the volunteers to feel discouraged and insignificant, and they leave the program.

One camper called the coordinator to complain, saying that other people have gifts and talents too. The coordinator invited this particular camper to be on the committee and gave her the assignment to collect the dues. She gladly accepted this assignment and gave it her best efforts. The coordinator assured her that she was the best person for the job. That camper never complained again. She arrived early each day and sat in her car until camp time. She was a blessing to this ministry, but in her unhappy state she could have made it a bitter situation for the coordinator, the staff, and the other campers.

We realized early on that we could not offer a stipend to the senior staff, but that we also needed a junior staff of young people who would set up the area for camp, greet and meet the campers with their bags, canes, walkers, and wheelchairs and assist them in stepping onto the sidewalk from the parking lot, help the campers to the washroom facilities, assist the caterer in the kitchen, serve lunch and help with cleanup afterwards, and help with games and wherever else needed. We decided that they needed to complete applications, to be trained, to get to work on time, to follow directions, and to be responsible to stay on task. We paid them for their service and docked them for being late or leaving early.

The experience of senior camp was most rewarding for both the campers and the staff. The kitchen workers loved their ministry to the campers, as did the volunteers who came in to teach crafts. As staff members grew older and were no longer able to serve, we recruited new staff as needed.

A Look at One Senior Camp

The following schedule shows what a typical camp day looked like for the first two weeks. In later weeks, we had a fifties parade of fashions, crafts, a discussion on living with diabetes, and a guest speaker from the circuit court of our county.

Week 1	9:00 AM - ALL-STAFF ARRIVAL			
	9:45	Assembly		ALL
	10:00	Worship in song and prayer		JD, MM, CD
	10:10	Meditation: Josh 1:7–9		DP
	10:20	Exercise		DCT
	10:30	"My Life, My Story"		Dr. BH
	11:30	Introductions and sharing		ALL
	12:00	Lunch		Caterer & Junior Staff
	1:15	Fun time	Bowling competition	MM & Junior Staff
			Hone-in-one (golf) competition	JS/JD & Junior Staff
	1:50	Announcements and closing		The Coordinator

Week 2	9:00 AM - ALL-STAFF ARRIVAL		
	9:45	Assembly	ALL
	10:00	Worship in song and prayer	JD, MM, CD
	10:10	Meditation: Deut 31:6	Dr. PB
	10:20	Exercise	DCT
	10:30	Dental health for seniors	Dr. KO
	11:00	Putting your house in order	Attorney RR
	12:00	Lunch	Caterer & Junior Staff
	12:45	Community technology liaison (utilities)	Citizens Utility Board
	1:15	Fun time — Bowling competition	MM & Junior Staff
		Fun time — Hole-in-one competition	JS/JD & Junior Staff
	1:50	Announcements and closing	The Coordinator

Record Keeping

Record keeping is most valuable for your organization, whether ministering to the sick and shut-ins or in another area of ministry. Although staff are a trusted group of Christians, tracking what is earned and what is spent is highly important. In order to keep registration fees as low as possible for our campers, we raised funds.

One of the most profitable fundraisers we had was a business fair with fish dinners. We sold tables and space to vendors; that was all clear money. Each staff member was asked to raise a minimum of $100 in dinner sales to members of the church and in their communities. During the time of the business fair, we had a volunteer chef who prepared fish dinners. The pleasant aroma brought people inside to purchase dinner. A great time of food, fellowship, and shopping was beneficial to all.

For our fundraiser we needed to track how many tickets were sold and how much money was raised versus how much expense we had. Although sheets were distributed to staff to indicate the names of purchasers and how many dinners they sold, the coordinator prepared a brief summary and reconciliation statement indicating all income and expenses and listing each check that was written along with a description of what it was for. We did the same for income, listing who turned in the money, how much money, and what it was for.

A simple table we used looked something like this:

Income			Prior Year	Expenses					
Date	Amt.	Descr.	Acct. Balance	Date	Amt.	Payee	Check #	Descr.	Balance

NOTE: This table is basic and would need to be adjusted for your specific use.

Registration for Seniors

It is highly suggested that the sick, shut-ins, and seniors register for church activities. With HIPAA (the Health Insurance Portability and Accountability Act) being enforced by law in the United States, there are so many things that staff may not be able to do when a church guest becomes ill. If a person loses consciousness, information is needed. For example, when our staff registered campers, we asked for the name of the nearest of kin, this person's relationship to the camper, and the telephone numbers where she or he could be reached during the hours of camp. Staff and even paramedics are helpless without certain information. A list of your guest's prescribed medications can also be helpful. The information obtained may be as extensive as you wish it to be. It may also include the guest's preferred hospital, and her or his doctor's name and telephone number is helpful. You should study the latest regulations to determine what you can and cannot do.

Resources and Services Available to Older Adults

There are numerous online resources providing valuable information in caring for seniors. For those residing in the United States, the Administration for Community Living (ACL) offers an eldercare locator website (see eldercare. acl.gov) that includes a wealth of information, including a searchable database linking users to unbiased information and resources that are available at the state and community level. The database includes state agencies on aging, area agencies on aging, aging and disability resources centers, aging information and referral programs, and special-purpose information and assistance resources for legal services and elder abuse prevention.

For links to the various U.S. state offices on aging and disability, see https://healthyaging.net/information/state-state-links-offices-aging-disability/.

Writing a Mission Statement

A mission statement serves to explain briefly and clearly the goals, purpose, and work of an organization. Assuming that a ministry to the sick, shut-ins, or seniors is connected with a local church, the mission statement of this ministry should be in agreement with that of the church. It should include who you are and what you do—not what you envision but your purpose for being.

One church's mission statement reads as follows:

XYZ church exists to make, mature, and multiply disciples of Jesus Christ, through the power of the Holy Spirit, for the glory of God.

- *We make disciples* through sharing the good news of Jesus with our words and living out the implications of the good news of Jesus in our lives.
- *We mature disciples* through growing in our understanding and application of the good news of Jesus in our lives.
- *We multiply disciples* through planting churches in new neighborhoods and throughout the world.

For the senior adult ministry of XYZ Church, the mission statement should be in line with this. Here's how the ministry's mission statement might read:

The mission of the XYZ Senior Adult Ministry is as follows:

- We lead others to Christ through sharing the Word of God to the sick and shut-ins in homes, hospitals, and nursing homes.
- We teach the Word of God through weekly Bible studies in senior-resident apartment buildings.
- We encourage senior members to each bring a guest to Bible study.
- We meet monthly for community, fun, food, fellowship, and exercise.

Goals of a Ministry to Shut-Ins or Seniors

When a basketball player finds himself fouling out in several consecutive games, it is time for him to set a goal to play without being the one who fouls. If he finds that he is less productive at making points either from the free-throw line or while running, he should set another goal to not just get better but to make a decided amount of points per game within a certain period based on what he has been doing in the past. To meet that goal means he has to set aside a dedicated amount of time or develop a particular schedule that is reasonable and workable to reach proven success. He must also remember that the goal must be measurable; once it is reached, he can establish a larger goal.

SMART goals are designed to help an individual, group, organization, or ministry break down a task into specific steps to complete in order for the main task to be achievable. The SMART concept was developed by George Doran, Arthur Miller, and James Cunningham in the early 1980s. If interested, you may want to do more research on the topic. Following is a general review of its basic elements.

SMART goals are:

- *Specific*—precise and detailed
- *Measurable*—capable of being measured or perceived
- *Attainable*—achievable
- *Realistic*—practical or possible
- *Timely*—given at an opportune or appropriate time

In a church or Christian organization, your goals should also be biblically based and God-approved for your particular situation and context. Another church may have been successful in completing a goal that your church is not equipped to do. A goal may fit all of the above criteria, but if God is not in it and he did not direct you to do it, you should not pursue it.

In visiting the sick and shut-ins, the leaders in our group decided that our goal would be to minister to a minimum of fifteen people on the third Sunday after church. That was *specific*. With twelve leaders, it was *measurable*, *attainable*, *realistic*, and *timely*. Some leaders could visit several persons in one hospital or nursing home. We spent a maximum of twenty minutes with each person, sharing a song, scripture, prayer, Communion, and a closing song. We chose not to sit and get comfortable. It was our mission to allow a few minutes for small talk while leaving the person intact or better. Some lonely and talkative saints required thirty minutes of time. For groups who had to travel further, they would be assigned one person only. The coordinator would often take the heavier load in order to accomplish our set goal. Even though the arrangements had been made the prior day, sometimes the people we went to see were unavailable, and we had to account for this.

For our senior camp, the coordinator worked with the leadership team to plan a well-rounded program for four weeks, four hours each week. That meant strategic planning to cover the time period from 9:00 AM to 3:00 PM including set-up in the morning and clean-up in the afternoon by the adult and teen staff. Our guests spent four quality hours from devotional to dismissal. We accomplished our goals weekly because the staff members were educated in their specific assignments, including a registrar, kitchen staff, craft staff, a secretary, a treasurer, and a staff person to supervise the teens. The coordinator was deliberate in sharing with outside speakers the importance of maintaining their timeframes and provided a schedule and a reminder telephone call before their appointed time to present.

When we set goals, it is the beginning to being successful in our efforts. It assigns purpose and accountability to the mission at hand. For ministry to the sick, shut-ins, seniors, or others, our goals should tie into the overall goals and missions of the church or larger organization.

In Luke 14:28 (NIV), Jesus said, "Suppose one of you wants to build a tower. Won't you first sit down and estimate the cost to see if you have enough money to complete it?" Basically, we need to know the who, what, when, where, why, and how of the total project or goal we are contemplating with prayer and God's guidance. There are times we might decide to do something without taking into consideration all of the necessary steps and when it fails, we need to look back at who and what caused the failure. Jesus' words suggest that we count the cost and the consequences before building any tower.

Here are some biblical examples of situations where goals were given:

- Matthew 28:18–20 (NIV)—"Then Jesus came to them and said, 'All authority in heaven and on earth has been given to me. Therefore go and make disciples of all nations, baptizing them in the name of the Father and of the Son and of the Holy Spirit, and teaching them to obey everything I have command-ed you. And surely I am with you always, to the very end of the age.' " In this situation, all of the SMART criteria were met. Jesus left nothing to the imagination; after baptizing, the disciples would not be left standing around wondering what to do next. He said specifically what to do and what his role would be in it all. He gave specific directions. If they had questions, they could have asked. The directives were clear and without question of what to do or in which order.

- Genesis 12:1–3 (NIV)—"The LORD…said to Abram, 'Go from your country, your people and your father's household to the land I will show you. I will make you into a great nation, and I will bless you; I will make your name great, and you will be a blessing. I will bless those who bless you, and whoever curses you I will curse; and all peoples on earth will be blessed through you.' " In this biblical example, all of the SMART criteria were not immediately met. Sometimes our faith is tested and we must follow God's word without ques-tion to see what the end will be. God did not give Abram all the components of specific, measurable, attainable, realistic, or timely goals here. He did not give him a timeframe, whereas SMART goals are designed to help you break down a task into specific segments that identify how to complete the steps in order for the task to be achievable. But remember, any goal God gives you is attainable and realistic, and it can be accomplished in his time.

Conclusion

Proverbs 16:9 (NIV) says, "In their hearts humans plan their course, but the LORD establishes their steps." The key to effective ministry to the sick, shut-ins, and seniors is to keep our hearts and minds aligned with God and allow the steps of our goals to be directed by the Lord. Keep God clearly in focus. If you do so, your life and your ministry will be a credit to him, to the church, and to the specific tasks he has entrusted to you.

About the Author

Rev. Linda L. Braggs, associate minister at Covenant Faith Church of God in Chicago, Illinois, is a biblical and inspirational storyteller. She loves to tell stories that challenge and inspire her audiences and seeks to be a blessing to each listener. She has served as a leader in senior adult ministry and is the current discipleship teacher at her church. She has a bachelor's degree in Applied Behavioral Science and a master's degree in Adult Education, both from National-Lewis University. Braggs has taught and led workshops and spoken in a variety of venues both locally and nationally. She has been blessed with two successful adult children (one deceased) and three brilliant and generous grandchildren.

Linda's favorite Bible verse, which expresses the goal of her life and ministry, is Colossians 3:23 (NIV): "Whatever you do, work at it with all your heart, as working for the Lord." Her desire is to see people of all ages know and serve God.

17. Prison Ministry
by Ben Santiago

I want to share with you my personal journey and how I got started in prison ministry. I was born in Puerto Rico. When I was a small child, my mother came to the United States to find work and left me in Puerto Rico in the care of my godparents. When I was five years old, she sent for me. I arrived in New York City by myself on an airplane.

My mother worked seven days a week and had a hard time making ends meet. There were times we were homeless; at other times we lived in homes with other people where we rented a room or even just a bed in a large room with several other people. Sometimes I only saw my mother once a week. We struggled to find a place to live that my mother could afford, so we moved around a lot.

My mother never learned to speak English, so she could not help me with my homework. At that time the schools did not have English-as-a-second-language curriculum, so I struggled greatly in my studies. I really wanted to learn, but I fell further and further behind. I didn't know it then, but I was later diagnosed as having attention deficit disorder and dyslexia.

Alcohol was readily available in our family, and at a very young age I began drinking any type of alcoholic beverage I could find. After we had a more stable place to live, my older brother joined us from Puerto Rico. He introduced me to marijuana, and I began using it daily. I would steal my lunch from the cafeteria and use my lunch money to buy drugs and would be high all day in school.

In the 1960s, the country started desegregating schools. As part of the desegregation effort, my friends and I ended up being bussed from our Hispanic ghetto neighborhood to a middle-class Caucasian neighborhood. It was at the white school that I started using harder drugs—pills, speed, LSD, PCP, etc. Getting high and hanging out in Central Park with the hippies was my pastime. Later I started using other drugs, including heroin. I began by just snorting it but ended up taking it intravenously, which resulted in sharing needles and using whatever drug I could get.

I had started praying to be free from my addiction. I went to many drug treatment programs, including a methadone maintenance program. As a juvenile, I was arrested for joyriding and also blamed for vandalizing a teacher's car. I was eventually sent to the Rikers Island Jail Complex for possession of marijuana.

I was grateful my mother was able to scrape up enough money from friends and relatives to bond me out.

My Start in Prison Ministry

After I was saved, I began talking with a local chaplain about my desire to minister within the prison system. The Lord began providing opportunities for me to serve in great and mighty ways. I was able to hold Bible studies and baptisms, serve Communion, preach the gospel, and see inmates one-on-one.

That initial experience opened doors for me to eventually become the senior chaplain for the Madison County Sheriff's Department Secure Detention Unit, Correctional Complex, Youth Center, and Work Release Program in central Indiana. Through my pastor, I was able to meet the county sheriff; he and I bonded and he asked me to start a different kind of ministry, with the churches in the community fully participating. I knew this was God's work.

The Importance of Prison Ministry

The goal of ministry in prisons or jails, as with evangelism on the streets, is to reach the lost in our communities. People who continue to commit crimes will eventually end up incarcerated. When those steel doors lock behind them, they are forced to face failures, wrong choices, bad associations, and harmful lifestyles, all of which have distanced them from God. They may be asking themselves questions such as, "How did I end up here? Is there a better way? Can I change my ways?" If these questions are to be answered and real change is to take root, seeds of faith must be planted and nurtured. That is where a prison or jail ministry comes in. The time is now for these inmates. You can become the light to introduce them to the love and forgiveness of Jesus Christ that they need and are searching for, leading them to God-centered and productive lives.

When churches become involved in prison ministry, it is good for the community as a whole. Sadly, the doors to the jail are quite often revolving doors. However, through effective prison ministry, we can bring hope to those who desperately need it. The community at large will reap the benefits of this transformation because it breaks the vicious and repetitive circle of crime. Prison ministry can help people replace the pain and disappointment in their lives with the hope, reconciliation, and forgiveness of God.

There is another good reason for churches to get involved. If we do not minister to these inmates, cults and various non-Christian religions and gangs can take hold and take advantage of them. When that happens, we lose precious opportunities in the prisons and jails. Evangelism is a very important part of the church, but especially in prison ministry.

Jesus said in Matthew 25:35–40 (NIV), " 'I was hungry and you gave me something to eat, I was thirsty and you gave me something to drink, I was a stranger and you invited me in, I needed clothes and you clothed me, I was sick and you looked after me, *I was in prison and you came to visit me.'* Then the righteous will answer him, 'Lord, when did we see you hungry and feed you, or thirsty and give you something to drink? When did we see you a stranger and invite you in, or needing clothes and clothe you? When did we see you sick or in prison and go to visit you?' The King will reply, 'Truly I tell you, whatever you did for one of the least of these brothers and sisters of mine, you did for me' " (emphasis added). Acts 16:25–34 tells of the miraculous experience of Paul and Silas in the Philippian jail, culminating with the salvation and baptism of the jailer and his household. Prison is a place where God operates to provide hope to those who are in dire need of it.

The Christian church should always be involved in bringing hope and salvation to those in jails and prisons, to those living in a place where it often seems the world, their family, and their friends have basically forsaken them. When inmates feel that everyone has given up on them—that is the time when Jesus steps in with his love and compassion through dedicated servants of the church.

Starting a Prison Ministry Program

If you are interested in forming a jail or prison ministry, first make sure this is something you feel that God is calling you to do. If so, start by making an appointment with the county sheriff, chief administrator, or jail commander. If possible, show unity by coming with a few other ministers from the community because there is always strength in numbers.

Explain not only the spiritual benefits the program would have but also the improved inmate behavior within the facility that can result. Expound upon the benefit to the community, as almost all inmates at some point in time will be released and return back to active roles in society. It is a benefit to community safety overall to have the inmates come out better than they went in. Without significant life change, there is a risk to the safety of the community as well as added expense to taxpayers to have to incarcerate these persons again.

Explain how it would be beneficial for the prison or jail to have a program such as you are suggesting. All inmates have a right to practice their religion while incarcerated, and this will help to provide that opportunity. If there is not a chaplain serving at the facility, another staff member may be assigned to oversee this area; that person may or may not have the religious calling to do so and may only devote minimal attention to the task.

When you present your program to officials, be sure to have a specific vision of what you want the program to achieve. Your goals may change over time, but it is good to start with a clear plan. Know how you are going to be funded. Will it be all volunteer, will it be funded through the institution itself, or will it be a non-profit and operated through grants, donations, and fundraisers? It is a good idea to familiarize yourself with how such programs are run by shadowing another prison ministry to see how they do things.

Preparing People for Prison Ministry

When people are seeking to be involved in prison ministry, they need to be aware that this area of ministry requires personal conviction. It is very important that they are sure of their salvation and are certain this is something God has called them to do—that they are not doing it because of pressure from someone else. Is there is a tug on the volunteer's heart to reach the lost? It is also important to know whether a potential volunteer has ever "been in the system"—in other words, whether he or she has been incarcerated. Someone who has served time in jail or prison has valuable experience that can help this person relate to inmates. If the volunteer has been incarcerated, it is important that this person has been out long enough to prove that he or she has truly changed, learned from past mistakes, and put the past behind. Depending on the person's past offense, I recommend a time gap of one to three years. If the individual can go for that long without re-offending, there is good chance that he or she is serious about making the necessary life changes.

People who are going to become involved in this kind of ministry need to know that going to a prison is different from going to a jail. Jails and prisons have two distinctly different populations and settings. In general, inmates in a jail have often not been found guilty yet or have not yet been sentenced. If they have been sentenced, they are there for minor offenses and will often have sentences of a year or less.

Those who go to prison have almost always spent time in jail first. In prison, inmates have been found guilty and sentenced to serve time. Those sentences usually range anywhere from a couple of years to life.

Christians who will be ministering in a jail or prison setting have nothing to fear from the inmates. These men and women are looking for help. Volunteers will find that if they come to represent God's love and bring hope, a lot of the inmates will respect them.

It is very important that male and female volunteers be allowed to come in together. However, for safety purposes they should not visit one-on-one with offenders of the opposite sex. Inmates will often try to manipulate volunteers, so it is good to avoid situations that could lead to opposite-sex attractions. A more seasoned volunteer should oversee new volunteers who may be naïve and easily manipulated.

Varieties of Opportunities

There are many opportunities to get involved in prison or jail ministry. These institutions will often appoint a pastor or ordained minister as an official chaplain. Some qualifying factors might include training or a degree in biblical teaching, a desire to work with inmates, previous certification as a chaplain, and knowledge or experience in any area of law enforcement.

Serving as an official chaplain is a wonderful thing to do, but it is not the only way to be involved. You and members of your church can volunteer to help by leading a chapel/worship service through an existing chaplaincy program. If the jail or prison already has a chaplain, you can talk to this person about how you and your church can become involved, if that is something you feel led to do.

Those who minister in jails and prisons can also serve law enforcement officers and correctional staff. In today's world these men and women, as well as their families, face extreme situations and pressures almost continually. Officers put themselves in harm's way every day and endure stress that many of us cannot comprehend. Those who serve in prison ministry can meet their needs by coming alongside them and helping them work through some of their professional problems and issues, crises in their own families, and spiritual struggles. Law enforcement officers and institutional staff need someone they can confidentially talk to without fear of any repercussions.

In addition to group chapel settings, you can also volunteer to see prisoners on an individual basis. They will request one-on-one meetings with a chaplain for prayer or spiritual counsel. This is a wonderful way to speak with someone on a personal level regarding his or her relationship with Christ.

Prison Rules and Regulations

I would be remiss if I did not address some of the basic rules and regulations of the prison system. These are things that are applicable for all persons who work or serve in prisons. Knowing these rules and regulations can help those who wish to be part of a prison ministry avoid some of the pitfalls and predicaments associated with this area of service.

Those who step forward to volunteer for prison ministry should live up to the responsibility of their volunteer role. Volunteer work is not something that can be done as an afterthought when there is nothing more exciting to do; rather, it is a responsibility that requires a definite allotment of time, energy, and intelligence, the desire to do it, and adequate preparations.

Just as with a paid job, volunteer positions also need clearly specified guidelines. Detailed in the following section are some pertinent rules and codes of conduct for successful prison ministry. These are culled from my own experience and context of prison ministry and may not apply in all situations:

As a volunteer prison worker,

- Be honest and genuine at all times. Be friendly, and enjoy the experience yourself.
- Be optimistic about life in general, but do not encourage any unrealistic goals or attitudes.
- Respect the confidential aspect of your assignment and the dignity and privacy of the inmates with whom you work.
- Regard each offender as a whole individual, not merely as a delinquent person.
- Respect any cultural, ethnic, religious, and personal differences. Be flexible, making allowances for an inmate's abilities.
- Be present and on time for every commitment you make. If you find yourself unable to meet an obligation, notify the group leader as far in advance as possible.
- Know the rules of the facility you are visiting and obey them. Some routine actions may be prohibited.
- Ask the institution staff about anything you do not understand. Do not harbor any doubts or frustrations.
- Inform the institution staff if you have a friend or relative incarcerated in the facility where you will be serving.
- Do not argue with the institution staff or an inmate about anything. If a problem should arise, consult with your volunteer leader or the on-site chaplain.
- Be a part of the team. Be willing to accept supervision and training from the team leader, on-site chaplain, or others. Your cooperation is important.
- Do not show partiality to one inmate over another.
- Report immediately any unusual behavior, activity, or problem you observe.
- Dress appropriately and according to the facility's dress code.
- Do not degrade other religious beliefs to favor your own.
- Do not discuss with inmates anything regarding jail conditions, jail policies, or any controversial subject matter pertaining to corrections.

168

- Do not show your surprise at anything you see.
- Do not discuss an inmate's charge (what that person has been convicted of).
- Do not traffic materials in or out of the facility; it's against the law.
- Do not deliver or carry messages to or from inmates.
- Do not purchase anything for inmates.
- Do not send money for inmates without the proper approval from prison staff.
- Show empathy toward inmates and their concerns. Empathy is the ability to relate to another and understand his or her feelings without emotional involvement.
- Do not show emotional reaction toward an inmate's attitudes and convictions.
- Do not become emotionally involved with an inmate. Immediately notify your volunteer leader or the on-site chaplain if you suspect an offender has become emotionally involved with you.
- Do not discuss any information pertaining to an inmate with the public.
- Do not under any circumstances discuss your personal life with an inmate.
- Do not permit yourself to listen to explicit sexual conversations being verbalized by an inmate. Inform your leader if this should occur.
- Do not touch an inmate or allow this person to touch you.
- Do not spend an excessive amount of time with any one inmate. It is important to monitor yourself to ensure time spent with one inmate is not significantly greater than that spent with others.

The development of a mutually respectful relationship with an inmate is important. The primary way to achieve this kind of rapport is to display responsible adult behavior, which includes setting limits and treating all inmates with respect. Communicate to inmates that you believe they are capable of becoming fully functioning and law-abiding citizens. Let them know there are no acceptable excuses for breaking the rules, and give them credit when they have done well.

Inmates will frequently view female volunteers in stereotypical roles, developing fantasies about their relationship with these volunteers. These fantasies may range from seeing the volunteer as a "mother" to seeing her as a girlfriend or sex partner. Inmates must be given a message that such fantasies are not reality. If you are viewed as a mother figure, make it clear that while such wishes are normal, you are not going to fulfill that role.

Sometimes you may encounter whistles, stares, and obscene remarks when you are around inmates. In general, you should ignore this behavior and immediately report it to your volunteer leader, staff, or the on-site chaplain.

Compliments, as opposed to explicit sexual remarks, may occur. You should respond by indicating that although the sentiment is appreciated, you would prefer that personal remarks not be made.

Volunteers must beware of becoming overly familiar or engaging in fraternization with inmates. Examples of such behavior include talking about your personal life, "relaxing the rules" for certain inmates, having certain inmates routinely do special favors for you, talking to inmates about other volunteers or prison staff, contacting family or friends of an inmate, or contacting the victim or family members of the victim of the inmate's crime. Any of these activities can lead to a volunteer violating prison rules or becoming a victim of harassment or blackmail, and may result in this person's termination as a volunteer. You can communicate with offenders with respect, concern, and kindness without becoming overly familiar.

Conclusion

God used my past experiences to prepare me for his call to serve in prison ministry. Whatever your own experiences, if God is calling you to serve in this way or to lead your congregation in such a ministry, may he bless you and use your gifts and your passion to share the good news of Jesus Christ with men and women who desperately need to hear it.

About the Author

Ben Santiago is the executive director, senior chaplain, and founder of the Madison County Sheriff's Department chaplaincy program in central Indiana. A graduate of Redeemer Bible Institute of Brooklyn, New York, he and his wife, Tammy, were married in 1983. God blessed their marriage with a lovely daughter, Lydia Joy.

After being ordained in the Church of God, Ben continued his education with a variety of training and certifications in leadership and development, including a Bachelor of Science in Addictions Counseling and Christian Ministries from Indiana Wesleyan University.

While living in Indiana, God has blessed Ben both physically and in ministry for him. In 1986, he was the recipient of a kidney transplant. In 2015, God allowed new medications to be developed that cured him of Hepatitis C. Ben is grateful for the ways the Lord has used him and the doors God has opened for prison ministry in Indiana.

PART V:

Threats and Challenges of Pastoral Ministry

18. Considering Retirement
by Reginald G. Smith

A story is told about an avid golfer who came to his pastor and said, "You know how much I play golf. One of these days I am going to die, and I would like to know when that happens if I will be able to play a round of golf with God himself. If you can grant me that knowledge, I will give $250,000 to the church."

Not wanting to pass up such a generous gift, the pastor replied that he must search out relevant passages in the Bible as well as pray for an answer. Two days later he called his parishioner back and announced, "I have good news and bad news for you. The good news is that I prayed and prayed and read the Bible twice over, and I have it on good authority that when you die, indeed you will play the first round of golf with God himself. The bad news is that your tee-off time is Tuesday at 10:00 AM."[1]

It has been eleven years since I retired from active pastoral care of a congregation of the Church of God. For me, pastoral ending has been a new beginning. The knowledge and wisdom I have gained while reading credible sources of information for writing this chapter have left me wishing I had done this many years ago. The executive offices of the national church located in Anderson, Indiana, have been dealing administratively with retirement matters with a view of helping retirees. It is my hope in this chapter to include some personal and practical perspective on what it means to be a retired pastor. Many pastors before me have already initiated some of the suggested strategies related to timing, transition, succession, and post-retirement integration.

What Is Retirement?

Fundamentally, retirement is a time to end strongly and on a positive note. However, a pastoral leader's retirement has consequences that are not restricted to the retiree alone. Retirement has consequences for coworkers, co-leaders, spouses, and congregants. They are entitled to clear and timely communication so they can prepare to manage the resulting changes in their own lives.

The basic limited and outdated meaning of retirement is "to disappear or withdraw from active employment." That refers to a time when only men were laborers and retirement was introduced as a privilege and reward for hard work. Given the changes that have occurred in areas such as economics, life expectancy, and technology, as well as prevailing societal attitudes, there has been an emergence of alternative descriptions for retirement such as "the next stage," "the third chapter of life," "the encore years," and "second career."

In the United States, the Social Security Act of 1935 stipulated qualification for retirement at age sixty-five, but life expectancy at that time was just under sixty-two years of age. Retirement is progressively more a matter of adopting a process of reinventing oneself by embracing new opportunities and relationships. Television reporter Jane Pauley once said that retirement used to be a door marked "Exit" but now is more like a door that swings on a hinge, moving a person from one thing to something else. One recent advertisement said that retirement is paying ourselves for doing what we love.

Timing

The critical question that will not yield a quick answer is, *When should one retire?* In the U.S., this question may have been partially answered by legal qualification for Social Security. Non-western cultures value persons for their accumulated wisdom and experience, which usually correlate with advanced age—therefore, years don't matter as much as the "spirit" of those years.

One major consideration in retirement is whether the minister continues to be productive in ministry. I am always amazed at the level of patience and tolerance exhibited in the presence of chronically unproductive ministerial service in some sectors of Christendom. Some of that may be understandable given our congregational polity that promotes more subjectivity than objectivity in determining points of diminishing returns. Is the loved and well-intentioned minister capable of maintaining effective ministry?

In general, specified retirement age as such will not necessarily indicate the right time to retire. Budgetary considerations could be a strong determining factor, especially where a leader is unable to inspire optimism among financial supporters. Marginal productivity may be seen as disqualifying for continued leadership. However, in the final analysis, good relationships are indispensable like no other variable.

It should come as no surprise that one's call into Christian ministry has elements of mystery, since that third member of the Godhead—the Holy Spirit—is the person who initially lays the call upon one's heart. Others in the faith household may recognize and give witness to one's call, but the reality of that call is an internal spiritual happening. Given that fact, the timing of one's retirement bears the similar character of mystery. As long as a minister is in good standing with the members of the Godhead, no pastor, bishop, overseer, ministry colleague, or other church official can legitimately witness to the timing of a minister's retirement. If you feel required by others to retire, that will have some negative consequences for your self-esteem. The legitimate witness is that inner voice only, who says, "It's time."

For some understandable reasons, a minister may need to work beyond his or her point of diminishing returns, especially where there are forgivable resource deficits. Be that as it may, God's pastoral servants who have had a record of anointed stewardship do know beyond doubt when retirement is in God's will as well as in the best interests of the pastorate and the Kingdom. They sense the Spirit's "inner voice" leading them to consider this change for the future. The time does come when pastors need to see the church without themselves in a leadership role. If they don't, they may be hanging on and going "past their exit," so to speak.

One should not delay his or her retirement in order to experience, for instance, a delayed church construction project. Each of God's ministerial servants has an allotted time of service. When that time has passed, his servant should graciously make way for younger persons to have their time of service and not create a clog in the servanthood pipeline.

Planning

Successful retirement for a minister occurs when the individual is able to thrive vocationally, socially, physically, and spiritually in retirement. The issue of personal-professional identity looms large, especially where the retiree has not exited the precincts of his or her successor's pastoral reach. For financial reasons, it may not be practical for a retiree to move out of state or a "safe" distance away.

Ideally, the best option for a pastoral retiree is to have absolutely nothing to do with his or her successor's administration, even where the retiree has enjoyed healthy previous relationships and has finished well. The temptation to offer direct or indirect intervention where your successor is having understandable adjustment challenges needs to be stoutly resisted unless one's successor requests problem-solving assistance.

Experience has taught many of us retired pastors that our successors in this contemporary era have no felt need for us or for our help. They manifest a certain independence which bespeaks their conviction that what they bring to their pastoral responsibility is superior and will be much more productive in terms of assimilation and church growth—and in some cases, depending on their level of giftedness and anointing, this could be true. Any kind of intervention, no matter how well intentioned, could be interpreted as the retiree's failure to "release the steering wheel," and that has potential for unhealthy relationship strains.

Kiplinger's publishes an annual retirement planning guide with contents that have been found to be helpful in terms of personal, physical, relational, and social matters. Retirees need to keep their historical friendships active. Retirement seldom requires a termination of past key relationships with either clergy or laity. Actually, a minister's spiritual health is to a great extent nurtured by having good relationships within and without one's sphere of influence. Retirement would be a drab existence without the continuation of existing close relationships, keeping in mind that physical "one-to-one" presence is not always necessary for the maintenance of vital relationships. A retiree should not expect to be loved and respected just because he or she is a retired pastor. That expectation would be unrealistic in the absence of historical if not new relationships.

Pastoral/Spiritual Concerns

There are indeed some situations where retirees cannot help being confronted with anxiety-producing situations. Author Steve Harper cites successors who make changes quickly while feeling no need for advice or knowledge about the congregation's history and its programs. The retired pastor is already wrestling with the sense of losing his or her worshipping community, and now members from the congregation struggle with the adjustments in light of the felt "loss" of the retired pastor they have known and loved. Rather than yield to the temptation to engage in behind-the-scenes maneuvering, retirees need to explore ways of reinventing themselves by finding roles that will bring new joys and satisfaction.[2] The retiree should never yield to being tempted or goaded to start another church to "comfort the afflicted," especially where one claims that one's retirement was divinely directed.

At retirement, one is still able to make decisions, develop plans, and make meaningful adjustments; therefore, personal growth does not need to stop. Retirement is no longer considered a retreat into a holding pattern until death. During his professional heyday, Walter Reuther asserted that a retiree was someone too old to work and too young to die. Rather than face the situation with pessimism, retirement needs to be planned for and approached with optimistic anticipation. It is not an event but an ongoing process.

It makes all the sense in the world to start thinking about retirement while a minister is functioning "at the top of his or her game," so to speak, usually at least ten years ahead of an anticipated date. This permits time for realistic planning, since even the best objectives are subject to unknown developments.

In 1994, the congregation I served hired the church's first full-time associate to take leadership in the area of youth ministry with the unmentioned goal of possible transition and succession to the role of senior pastor. This was done without making any premature commitment, since a track record was yet to be in place. As it turned out, this associate took a pastorate in a northern city in 1999. His separation was therapeutic for all concerned. By late 2001 our second associate arrived, following visits during which he was given exposure across a range of ministry areas. We were excited about his prospects with us. From the beginning this associate was made aware of the coming transition and his possible succession. As it turned out, this associate's tenure ended three years later with separation that was regrettably less than therapeutic for the twenty-four-year-old church, my wife, and myself.

What is the derivative wisdom here as far as retirement is concerned? First of all, prevailing circumstances demanded a retirement delay for me until the end of 2007. My third and relatively young successor spent approximately two years in pastoral formation, and is now doing very well ten years after succeeding me.

Second, while it is in some ways laudable to bring a potential successor on staff with a view of this person "learning the ropes" and registering acceptability with congregants, an incumbent should never mention a date of possible retirement. Offering a retirement date before ascertaining its validity and practicality sets up the potential for encountering some of the most distasteful and sometimes repetitive queries that the successor could make of the pastor: "When are you going to retire? Do you know how many people will leave here if I leave?"

Inasmuch as it is wise and perhaps visionary to start planning one's retirement even when there is no demonstrated reason to accelerate planning, such planning is actually a hedge against being overtaken by crises. Nathan and Beth Davis suggest that "successful retirement planning usually requires a considerable amount of time…. Some individuals begin retirement planning only after a crisis or illness forces them into an earlier than expected retirement."[3] It is therefore preferable to base one's retirement on wellness rather than illness or other crises. Even if an unexpected crisis occurs, the existing plan ought to be updated rather than discarded. At least it ought to be periodically revisited and updated to keep abreast of related changes.

Physical/Health Concerns

Certainly we might anticipate maintaining adequate income as a major factor in how much we will enjoy our retirement years, but the condition of our physical bodies—obesity, diabetes, heart issues, and other things—can also present difficult challenges during retirement.

The issue of healthcare merits some consideration. If a retiree elects to remain in the locale where he or she was serving, continued use of healthcare providers and services there is advisable. It might be wise to enquire whether one's physician will be keeping his or her practice. In the event the retiree contemplates relocation, he or she should request a physician's referral, since healthcare providers will often accept patients more readily if they are recommended by another doctor.

At age sixty-five, citizens and permanent residents in the United States may qualify for Medicare. One might be ordinarily apprehensive about negotiating the sprawling and complex bureaucracy associated with this benefit. However, some patients have reported that Medicare enrollment has become more user friendly. One Medicare advantage is that upon choosing a health insurance company that is connected with Medicare, the monthly premium is paid directly to the insurance company with no extra payment required of the enrollee. Also, during the enrollment period (October 15 to early December), your coverage continues automatically if you remain with your same doctor.

One excellent source of information regarding diet is www.choosemyplate.gov. Ministerial couples ought to be first among those who stop denying that being overweight harms their health and longevity. Risk factors associated with poor nutrition and lack of exercise increase greatly after age sixty-five. Retirees who maintain a sedentary middle-age diet and exercise regimen almost guarantee a variety of resulting physical problems.

It is an item of paramount importance that ministers adopt a healthy regimen during their working years if they would enjoy great health in their later years. Using the analogy of maintaining a new automobile, careful attention is given to timely engine oil and transmission oil changes in the interest of satisfactory engine performance for years to come. Although the years of an automobile's usable life pale in comparison with the human lifespan, this principle still holds. The enjoyment of great health during retirement is in close correlation to the excellent quality of health care secured during working years. Conversely, the longer it takes to adopt a healthy lifestyle, the greater the price that must be paid in facing health afflictions in one's senior years.

In regards to diet, a beginning practice is the eating of smaller portions than we used to eat and ingesting menu servings that are compatible with good health. An occupational hazard that confronts pastors is the number of invitations to public and private events where tasty meals and delicious desserts are served. Pastors need to take responsibility for regulating their food consumption preventively, especially when they know they are at risk for consuming certain items. They will do very well refusing to live with the "eat, drink, and be merry, for tomorrow we die" perspective.

What About Your Spouse?

One aspect of retirement that requires extremely close consideration is its impact upon the retiree's spouse. A happy marriage is a critical factor in making a positive adjustment, especially where the spouse is a female who has been substantially involved with her husband in pastoral effectiveness. The referenced impact has definite implications for their future relationship. In *Stepping Aside, Moving Ahead*, Steve Harper mentions the following items for careful consideration:

- Will my spouse continue to work after I retire?
- Can we create separate space at home for each of us?
- How will I foster life in my spouse and vice versa?
- How will we share household responsibilities?
- What do we look forward to doing together?
- Do we have a friendship network beyond ourselves?
- Will family be helpful or problematic?
- How can previous life changes help us?
- What have we learned from previous life changes that can help us now?

The objective is to certify the existence of a larger context for retirement. Upon announcing a decision to retire, outside assistance may also be explored in order to certify existence of a social network.

Some further questions for consideration:

- Whom do we know to have retired well?
- Whom may we be able to turn to for professional advice?
- What local, state, and federal resources will we be able to access?
- Who is the lawyer with whom we may discuss legal matters?
- Do we have a financial consultant?
- Does our church group or denomination have resources for our help as retirees?

Conclusion

While God's call to service never ends, there may come a day when it is time to retire from full-time vocational ministry. My prayer for you is that such a day of pastoral ending would be a time of new beginnings in your life, in your relationships, and in your service to the Lord.

About the Author

Reginald G. Smith is the son of Reginald and Anna Smith, who were among the first ministerial students to be trained by American missionaries for leadership in the Church of God in Jamaica, West Indies. He received his education at Mico Teachers College in Kingston, Jamaica; Anderson University in Anderson, Indiana; the New York University Graduate School of Social Work; Union Theological Seminary in New York City; and the Barry University Graduate School of Philosophy and Theology in Miami, Florida.

Dr. Smith was in pastoral ministry for thirty-two years, beginning in Harlem, New York. In 1980 he launched the Church of God of West Broward in Plantation, Florida, leading that church until his retirement in 2007. He continues to serve ecumenically as a preacher, a seminar leader, and a resource person for churches seeking to recruit pastoral successors.

Pastor Reggie's wife and partner in ministry, Carol Ann, went to her eternal reward in 2014. They were blessed with two sons, Courtney and Reginald Todd; two grandchildren, Courtney Jr. and Kendall; a daughter-in-law, Andrea; and an adopted daughter, Janice. Following divine leading, Reggie married Bernadette Bell, a happy wife and wonderful woman of God.

1. Daniel A. Roberts and Michael E. Freidman, *Clergy Retirement: Every Ending a New Beginning for Clergy, Their Families, and Congregants* (Eugene, OR: Wipf & Stock, 2017), 29–30.

2. See Steve Harper, *Stepping Aside, Moving Ahead: Spiritual and Practical Wisdom for Clergy Retirement* (Nashville: Abingdon Press, 2016).

3. Nathan Davis and Beth Davis, *Finishing Well: Retirement Skills for Ministers* (Springfield, MO: Nathan Davis, 2008), 42.

19. Resolving Conflict

by Alvin Lewis

The word *conflict* conjures up an array of negative and unholy thoughts, contradictions, and emotions in most of us. These negative thoughts and emotions are contrary to the values and virtues we teach in many of our churches. The purpose of this chapter is to help pastors, ministers, and laypersons understand the nature of conflict and discover appropriate and acceptable ways to triumph over it.

The Bible deals abundantly with conflict on many levels by identifying the various kinds of conflict and the reasons why conflict occurs. There are a number of words, in both the Old and New Testaments, that are used to describe conflict. For example, the Greek word *agō*, meaning "to lead," was used in reference to contests among athletes, such as the Greeks assembling for the Olympic and Pythian games. Paul used the term in 1 Timothy 6:12 and 2 Timothy 4:7 to describe the fight or contest for our faith. The word can also refer to "the inward conflict of the soul," with such internal conflict often resulting from an external conflict, and implies a contest against spiritual foes as well as human adversaries (see Col 2:1).

Another term used to help define the idea of conflict is the Greek word *eris*, which carries the notion of strife or quarrelling, especially a rivalry, contention, or wrangling, as in the church in Corinth (1 Cor 1:11). Then there is the word *paroxysmos*, often translated as "provoke" and inferring the sharpening of one's feeling or actions. It also denotes the effect of irritation, which can result in positive action (see Heb 10:24). A final word is *philoneikia*, which is a love of strife (*phileō*, "to love," *neikos*, "strife") and signifies an eagerness to contend (see Luke 22:24).

In this chapter I want to briefly cover four categories of conflict: individual, relational, spiritual, and global.

Individual Conflict

Individual conflict occurs when a person makes a deliberate choice contrary to God's Word and will, resulting in internal strife, negative consequences, and trouble with God. We see examples of this kind of choosing in the narrative about Adam and Eve. After receiving clear instruction from God, this couple made a decision to exercise a choice that was contrary to God's command. The Epistle of James speaks to the issue of such bad choices when it states, "If anyone, then, knows the good they ought to do and doesn't do it, it is sin for them" (James 4:17, NIV). James also points out that the consequences of our choices can lead to death: "After desire has conceived, it gives birth to sin; and sin, when it is full-grown, gives birth to death" (James 1:15, NIV).

Relational Conflict

Relational conflict is what takes place between two or more persons—in our context, within a church congregation. It may happen when there are warring factions in the church whose values, traditions, and philosophies clash. Sadly, our churches struggle daily with this kind of conflict. As pastors, ministers, and leaders, we need to work toward turning these negative situations into positive ones. May we all take heed to Paul's words to the Philippians when he wrote, "Do everything without grumbling or arguing, so that you may become blameless and pure, 'children of God without fault in a warped and crooked generation.' Then you will shine among them like stars in the sky" (Phil 2:14–15, NIV). Paul also wrote, "Finally, brothers and sisters, whatever is true, whatever is noble, whatever is right, whatever is pure, whatever is lovely, whatever is admirable—if anything is excellent or praiseworthy—think about such things. Whatever you have learned or received or heard from me, or seen in me—put it into practice. And the God of peace will be with you" (Phil 4:8–9, NIV).

Spiritual Conflict

Spiritual conflict can apply to an individual or to a group of individuals. This kind of conflict is mainly the outgrowth of issues we have with God and his Word. Spiritual conflict arises when we try to circumvent the truth of God and live by our own carnal standards. As humans, let us keep in mind that no matter how far we stray from the standards God has established, he will never compromise his divine principles. I am a firm believer that God does not engage in the game called *compromise*.

Equally important is the fact that God is spiritual in nature and must remain true to his own nature and character. We as human beings serve and are drawn to this spiritual God. Jesus affirmed this truth by stating, "God is spirit, and his worshipers must worship in the Spirit and in truth" (John 4:24, NIV). When God created us, he had a plan for our lives. But when we refuse to yield our lives to him, we miss the plan and the purpose he has established for us. Simply stated, this means that when we attempt to live outside of the plan God has for our lives, it can only lead to a life of defeat. Since God created us for his purpose, he wants us to have an authentic spiritual relationship with him.

God spoke about the kind and quality of relationship he desires for us to have with him through the prophet Jeremiah: " 'For I know the plans I have for you,' declares the LORD, 'plans to prosper you and not to harm you, plans to give you hope and a future. Then you will call on me and come and pray to me, and I will listen to you. You will seek me and find me when you seek me with all your heart' " (Jer 29:11–13, NIV).

Global Conflict

You might wonder what Christians have to do with global conflict. After all, such conflicts are created by governments, rulers, kings, and powerful people. But before we exempt ourselves from this type of conflict, I believe we need to think critically about the nature of global conflict. Remember that most, if not all, conflict starts with a choice.

The choices made by governments (whether good or bad ones) will involve the Christian and non-Christian alike. All the wars that were ever fought, most of the economic depressions we have experienced, the social injustices we have had to endure, and the racial and ethnic hatred people have suffered because of unfair laws and ordinances—the vast majority of these situations may all be laid at the doorstep of decisions made by governments.

Many people in power make decision based on expediency and the potential for personal gain rather than for the good of the people they govern. There are many choices governments and groups make that have far-reaching consequences for citizens who had no say so in those decisions, and this includes Christian citizens. As followers of Christ, we must learn to govern wisely because we have been given authority by God to represent his people.

Christians and Conflict

Why do Christians even find themselves in situations of conflict? If we love God, shouldn't every relationship and experience we have be peaceful? A little thought and reflection may prove that faith and conflict are not mutually exclusive concepts. The body of Christ has always struggled to deal appropriately with conflict; anyone who denies this has not read the Book of Acts or Paul's letters or studied church history. Conflict exists in most human and congregational relationships and will inevitably occur whenever people think differently and have incongruent needs or when their core values and beliefs are in conflict with one another. Spiritual and social conflict are a part of the human situation. Consequently, resolving conflict successfully becomes a duty and responsibility of every child of God.

Christian unity is a concept that has to be *worked out* and *worked on* in the church. Someone has aptly stated that, although we need each other, there are times we *needle* each other. The apostle Paul, who was a strong advocate of unity, found himself embroiled in personal and ecclesiastical disputes. A brief review of the New Testament will reveal several types of conflicts.

Conflicts about fair treatment. One of earliest illustrations of conflict in the young Christian church had to do with discontent expressed to the apostles by the Hellenistic Jewish Christians regarding the apparent neglect of their widows in the apportionment of daily food (Acts 6:1–7). We should note that when the apostles were confronted with this problem, they delegated its solution to those of lesser authority. They drew from the larger congregation by choosing seven men who were wise and were Spirit-filled, giving them responsibility to handle the situation.

Conflicts about religious and ethnic prejudice. Paul's tirade against Peter, recorded in Galatians 2:11–14, gives sufficient evidence of Paul's intolerance of Peter's hypocritical stance on eating with Gentiles. The language used by Paul was both caustic and corrective.

Conflicts over interpersonal disputes. Paul and Barnabas, two men who were dedicated to the cause of Christ, were divided over whether or not to take John Mark on their second missionary journey. Their differences over the issue became so great that the two men decided to sever their relationship, although only for a time (Acts 15:36–40; 2 Tim 4:11).

Conflicts arising from leadership disputes. The early church, like the modern church, also suffered from the "our-preacher-is-better-than-your preacher" syndrome. The deification of human leaders in the Corinthian church resulted in each faction openly campaigning for their chosen leader (1 Cor 1:11–17; 3:5–11).

Conflicts regarding authority. Some leaders in the first-century church, as in today's church, are quick to take a mile if given an inch. John was not afraid to identify and call out Diotrephes for unduly usurping authority and setting himself up as a "church boss" who put himself above others, did not acknowledge John's authority, spoke disparagingly against John, would not welcome other Christian leaders, and put those out of the congregation who differed with him (see 3 John 9–10).

How We May Profit from Church Conflict

There are important lessons to be learned even in the most trying crisis. Conflicts that arise within the body of Christ can sometimes be viewed as a sign of life and vitality. Although conflict often leads to a crisis, it can also become an opportunity for growth and enrichment in the lives of the persons involved and in the church itself. Let me set forth some ways in which we can benefit from situations of conflict.

Church conflict is a means of allowing anger to surface. Denying and disowning our feelings of anger is unhealthy and unholy. As Christians we should not deny our feelings, rather we should learn to deal with them honestly and openly. We can best deal with feelings of anger by facing them courageously and compassionately. This means that as followers of Christ we ought to be willing to own our anger and not try to hide it behind a cloak of deception. At the same time, as we admit to our anger and frustration, we should strive to overcome those negative feelings that would thwart positive relationships with other believers.

Church conflict ought to help us focus on central issues and not on personalities. The key to the resolution of any fight is an understanding of the issue or issues involved. Learning to center in on the issues helps us avoid the mistake of dealing in character assassination. All too often when we are angry over a situation, our feelings of hostility are directed toward the person or group on the opposing side. The consequence of such person-centered hostility is to circumvent the real issue and widen the rift in spiritual and interpersonal relationships. In contrast, an issue-oriented approach to church conflict seeks a common point of reference to which persons can direct their thoughts and energies. This can allow the central causes of the problem to be revealed and the persons involved to work toward a common solution.

Church conflict reveals individual and congregational weaknesses. Each of us wants to be seen, heard, understood, and loved. In some churches, however, these reasonable courtesies are not always extended to all members. Far too often compliments are one-sided and preferences are skewed toward the "favorite few." Individuals or groups who don't feel they are a part of the "in crowd" will sometimes leave the congregation or allow resentment to build toward those persons they perceive to be a threat to them. Cliques and factions are formed, and they can become warring enemies.

If individuals feel left out of congregational life for any reason, this should be sufficient cause for alarm on the part of the pastor and leaders—even the entire laity. A feeling of rejection by any church member could be a signal that there is a spiritual or structural weakness within the congregation. Therefore, it is wise and healthy for pastor and people to move quickly to address a break in relationships in the body of Christ. Finding ways of building a spirit of unity and inclusiveness is a task for the church to embark upon as faults are discovered. It must also be underscored that the church can only pursue such an undertaking as the people acknowledge their faults and work for true harmony.

185

Church conflict can become the channel through which we can solve perplexing problems. I am a firm believer that church fights can become the catalyst for solving some of our deepest problems. It is important to recognize our own wants and needs and be conscious about integrating them with the wants and needs of others. We should not be concerned over the fact that conflicts happen but instead focused on how we resolve those conflicts. The impact of a congregation coming together to solve problems can be creative, strengthening, and growth-producing.

Growing together as Christians in the body of Christ is a real challenge when differences have been discovered among us. But these differences and difficulties do not have to serve as barriers to Christian unity. Indeed, our differences and disagreements might point us to a need to grow and stretch as members of the church. Some dissentions could point out the need for more careful and helpful planning of church programs. Still other problems may cause the church to review its bylaws and other practices and policies that pertain to its members.

Conflict from a Pastoral Perspective

In his book *Managing Conflict in the Church,* David W. Kale cites a survey he conducted with forty pastors to identify the sources of conflict in their congregations. The following list reveals the twelve sources of conflict most commonly identified:

1. Communication problems
2. Differences over church mission and direction
3. Personality conflicts
4. Family conflicts (husbands and wives, parents and children, etc.)
5. Competition
6. Interpersonal relationships
7. Misunderstandings
8. Jealousy
9. "Turf protection"
10. Personal agendas
11. Lack of forgiveness
12. Distribution of work in the church

I am sure this list does not represent all the classifications of conflict situations. Nevertheless, it certainly identifies some key conflict areas that can require a major portion of a pastor's time and energy.

One observation I have made as a pastor and leader in the church is that when those in leadership seek to impose their goals on everyone in the congregation, it often results in unnecessary conflict. It is important for pastors and leaders to keep in mind that the goals of others in the church can enrich the direction we wish to go. Paul had to remind the church at Corinth that they were all members of one body (1 Cor 12:12–27).

Let me now move to the importance of biblical truth as a major value in addressing many conflicts in our churches. The Bible is the sacred book we acknowledge as the Word of God. It is the book we use for personal direction and inspiration. People gather in great numbers on Sunday mornings to hear preachers declare God's Word. We attend Bible classes through the week and gather at conventions annually to be renewed and inspired from the preaching and teachings of the Bible. If God's Word is essential in all of these settings and ways, why would we neglect to utilize it in our churches when faced with situations of conflict?

The following diagram is a tool to help understand how conflict originates and how it can accelerate into an uncontrollable relational disaster:

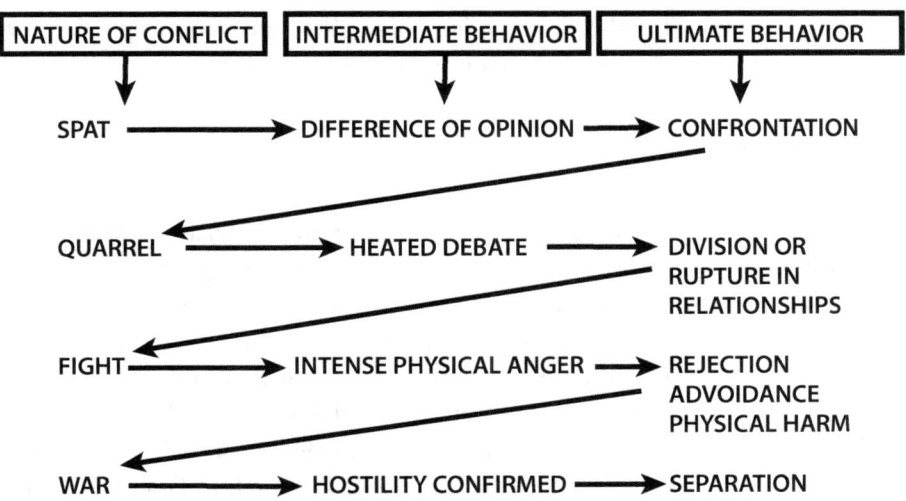

This diagram illustrates how a conflict moves from one stage to the next, building in intensity if not dealt with early on. A simple spat or disagreement in a congregation can lead to confrontation, with the expression of unkind behavior between associated parties. The conflict ends up taking on a life of its own, escalating at a quick pace when healthy solutions are not sought. Next, the members begin to quarrel with one another in heated debate, leading to sharp divisions and a rupture in relationships. If the conflict is still not addressed in a loving and redemptive way at this stage, attitudes take on a malicious and morose nature and the seditious seeds of a church fight are planted. When the conflict progresses this far, cool heads and Christian attitudes are no longer seen; relationships are significantly disrupted and physical altercations sometimes occur. The lines of combat are drawn in the sand and full-on war commences, with any and all behavior toward the enemy deemed as acceptable and justified. Just like in a military action, hostility is employed with the goal of destroying the enemy. Each side will create slogans, catchwords, and statements confirming that God is on their side. The separation of people leaving the church or of a church split is the end result.

Conclusion

It is possible to be a victor and not a victim of church conflict by being yourself at all times and not pretending to be anyone else. Try to always focus on issues and principles, not persons and personalities. Remember that your coworkers and church members need your honest input and not your fearful or hostile silence. Seek to always attribute good motives to those who disagree with you. Strive to address the problem and not attack the person. Resolving conflict successfully is your duty as you lead in the church. Times of conflict can become opportunities for healing and growth in your own life and in the church itself.

About the Author

Rev. Dr. Alvin Lewis earned his PhD (Adult Education and Adult Development), MS, and BS degrees from Kansas State University in Manhattan, Kansas, and his Master of Divinity degree from Garrett Evangelical Seminary in Evanston, Illinois. Dr. Lewis served as national director of adult and family life education/leadership development for the National Board of Christian Education of the Church of God, Anderson, Indiana, from 1974 to 1989. From 1989 to 1992 he was the executive director of the National Association of the Church of God, West Middlesex, Pennsylvania. From 1992 to 1999 he served as administrator and minister of pastoral care at the Vernon Park Church of God in Chicago, Illinois.

Lewis is the author of *Strategies for Educating African American Adults*; *Older Adult Resource Manual*; and *Directions: A Manual for Local Church Ministries*. He and his wife, Dr. Juanita Lewis, have three children: Alvin Vaughn, Lydia Janese, and Lystrelle Daneen.

20. Restoring Fallen Pastors

by Timothy J. Clarke

The subject of this chapter comprises a proverbial landmine that is both dangerous and difficult to navigate. The cause of this danger is both theological and ecclesiastical in that various denominations, fellowships, and reformations see things differently as to how or even if a "fallen" leader who has sinned should be restored.

Doctrinal Views of Salvation

At the very heart of this issue is one's view of *soteriology*, the doctrine of salvation. Some hold to a belief in what is often called "eternal security," also known as the Calvinist view or "the preservation of the saints." Those who adhere to this form of doctrine believe that once a person is saved, he or she cannot "lose" his or her salvation but is saved for eternity. In this view, Christians are secure in the work of Christ on their behalf eternally. Many who teach this doctrine also hold to the doctrine of "limited atonement." This is the teaching that God has predestined or predetermined who will be saved; only those who have been chosen will be saved, for they are eternally secure.

Another view of soteriology, most often found among those who embrace holiness teaching, is the idea of the "if" factor as it relates to our salvation. This teaching, based on the words of Jesus when he said, "If ye abide in me" (John 15:7, KJV), teaches that salvation is real, powerful, and lasting—but we must be *willing* to be kept.

The issue at hand here is this: *If one falls into sin, is it possible for this person to be pardoned and restored? Just what do we mean by restoration? How is it possible for one who has fallen into sin to be brought back to fellowship with God?* The landmine aspect of this issue can clearly be seen in some denominations or groups that simply do not allow a leader, e.g., a pastor, preacher, etc., who falls into sin to ever be restored to ministry and leadership. It is important to note that several of these groups have a soteriology of eternal security and yet no theology of restoration.

Let me make one more observation regarding this very sensitive area. There is also a distinctly different cultural dimension along this theological trail. Here is what I mean. In many African American churches, there is a greater willingness to forgive and restore a fallen leader than there is in the Euro-American context. This is purely anecdotal and based on observation and personal experience, but it cannot be dismissed or ignored altogether.

Three Components of Clergy Restoration

There are three parts of this subject of restoration that I would like to lift up for further consideration. The biblical record of failure on the part of Bible characters—in both the Old and New Testaments—is undeniably clear. The means and methods of their restoration require further exploration and explanation. And we need a model of restoration that is biblical and balanced, rooted in conviction and compassion.

I. The Biblical Record of Failure in the Lives of Bible Characters

For the purposes of this chapter I want to examine and explore some Bible personalities who are described and depicted as experiencing what can be called a moral failure or fall from grace. What is clear in each of their experiences is a unique crisis and challenge. Furthermore, there is no exception whether the subject is male or female. May I also add that this list is not exhaustive by any means. Let us examine some of the biblical characters who experienced falls and failures in their lives: Adam and Eve, Abraham, Noah, and others.

Adam and Eve

We often refer to the fall of Adam and Eve in Genesis 3 as the "original sin" or the "first fall." If we think about it, they were not just the first man and woman, husband and wife, father and mother—they were also the first leaders. They were given leadership roles at a level none of us are given. Adam and Eve were given dominion over all of creation, and their fall ushered in a new reality in our world order and in the lives of every person born since. Their fall was one of disobedience and rebellion, but it was brought on by fear, suspicion, and unchecked desire—things that all leaders need to fear and seek to avoid. When Adam and Eve sinned they sought to hide, to cover up, to place blame, as many leaders are prone to do in response to failure.

Abraham

Abraham is considered the father of the faithful, and he is a Bible figure revered and recognized by three of the major religions of the world. Yet with all that Abraham had going for him, we are still told that he had failures in his life. He lied to Pharaoh by saying Sarah was not his wife, but his sister (Gen 12). We are told that during Abraham's life he impregnated his wife's handmaid, and then in an act of what could at best be called cowardly he sent her and his son away to keep peace in his house (Gen 16; 21).

Noah

Genesis 9 tells us that even people and leaders of faith can have moments of doubt and failure. There is no doubt that Noah was a man of great faith and courage, and this is witnessed by his obedience to God in the building of the ark and his faith in the word of the Lord that it would rain and the world would be destroyed. Noah obeyed God, and he and his family were saved. Nevertheless, Noah had a dark side in his life. He got drunk after departing the ark and followed that up by cursing one of his sons, which brought conflict, controversy, and confusion—and continues to do so even to this day.

Moses

The account of Moses and his leadership covers much of the Book of Exodus and beyond in the Pentateuch. There is no doubt that he was one of the great leaders of the Bible, a lawgiver and liberator. And yet near the end of his life, Moses allowed his anger to boil over, and that outburst cost him going into and enjoying the Promised Land.

David

The books of First and Second Samuel tell us of that sweet singer of Israel, the man who led Israel with skill of hand and integrity of heart. There is no one like David in the pages of sacred writ, and yet his is not an unblemished story. For instance, there was his adulterous relationship with Bathsheba, his arranging the murder of Uriah, and his seldom-talked-about failure as a father and the devastation that brought to his family.

Peter

I think that it is safe to say that, whether we admit it or not, there is a little Simon Peter in all of us, in that all of us are a combination of passion and passivity, commitment and compromise, strength and struggle. Peter always meant well, and yet he did not always do well. Does this sound familiar? The failure of Peter (John 18) is well known, how he denied our Lord in the hour Jesus most needed friends. Peter's story reminds us to take heed of our own faults lest we fall. But despite Peter's terrible failure, Jesus restored him (John 21). On the Day of Pentecost, Peter was chosen to give the keynote message (Acts 2). God restored Peter, and he became one of most prominent leaders of the early church. Peter is still honored and revered by the modern-day church.

John Mark

I love the story of John Mark and how he was restored. We do not often talk about John Mark, and yet what we learn from him is that leadership failure is possible even when surrounded by the greatest leaders and mentors. Acts 13:13 tells us that, for some reason, John Mark walked away from ministry and abandoned his teammates. We learn from John Mark that no matter what our leadership title, we are still human and we all experience emotions and feelings that can move in and take over even when we do not expect them to do so. Acts 15 says that Paul was so disappointed in John Mark that he and Barnabas had a split over John Mark's cowardly conduct and never worked as a team again. And yet near the end of Paul's life and ministry, he wrote, "Take Mark, and bring him with thee: for he is profitable to me for the ministry" (2 Tim 4:11, KJV). What a powerful example of restoration, redemption, and forgiveness.

Now I am sure some of you may doubt that these were all failures or falls. That is the very reason I have included many of them, because we need to see that all failure is not sexual in nature; sometimes it is failure of leadership, courage, compassion, or direction, and when a leader fails in any of these areas it is costly and damaging.

Perhaps it is safe to say that ministry failure comes in all shapes and sizes, cultures and contexts.

II. THE BIBLICAL MEANS AND METHODS OF RESTORATION

The question I want to seek to answer next is this: Did God restore these people, and if so, how did he do it? The means and methods of restoration provide a true lesson in amazing grace. Let's look at a few of them.

Adam and Eve

With Adam and Eve, God drove them out of the garden, but he did not destroy them. He punished them, but he did not push them so far that they could not come back to him. He made clothes to cover them, representing the type of covering Jesus would later provide for sin, and he blocked the way to the garden so they could not come back in and eat of the tree of life and live forever. God further gave them children and continued their original assignment, albeit under far different circumstances.

Abraham

God honored Abraham and, as we have already acknowledged, Abraham is revered and recognized by three of the major religions of the world. He is still remembered as a man of faith and faithfulness.

Moses

God did not allow Moses to enter the Promised Land, but he did take him to the mount and allow him to see it. When Moses died, God himself buried Moses. The Book of Deuteronomy ends by saying, "There arose not a prophet since in Israel like unto Moses, whom the LORD knew face to face" (34:10, KJV). What a tribute—and what a God.

David

We know David is referred to as "a man after [God's] own heart" (Acts 13:22). God's challenge to the generations of kings after David lived was to "walk before me, as David thy father walked" (1 Kings 9:4, KJV). I am constantly amazed at what God chooses to remember and how he remembers us.

III. A BIBLICAL MODEL OF RESTORATION

I want to bring this chapter to a close by looking at a process by which restoration can take place. Even as I do so, let me say that the very fact we are looking at such a process suggests to me that failure on the part of a leader should never be taken lightly or dismissed flippantly but should be given every consideration of seriousness.

To restore a leader is serious business. One of the reasons the process must be taken seriously is because people need to have faith in the process and confidence in the restored leader. This cannot happen if the process has not been given adequate attention and consideration. Paul's words in Galatians 6:1 (KJV) give what many consider to be the definitive biblical word on reconciliation: "Brethren, if a man be overtaken in a fault, ye which are spiritual, restore such an one in the spirit of meekness; considering thyself, lest thou also be tempted."

This statement tells us some important things that warrant our consideration and observation:

- There is the possibility of a fall—"if a [person] be overtaken in a fault."
- There are specific persons who are to deal with the one who has fallen—"ye which are spiritual."
- There is a certain process employed in the restoration—"restore such [a person] in the spirit of meekness."
- The purpose for why the process is fulfilled—"considering thyself, lest thou also be tempted."

With this knowledge as a backdrop, let's look at how restoration can play out or be implemented.

There is a private aspect to the restoration process.

In this stage of the process, there is the admission or confession of the failure. This can be done to a trusted advisor, an accountability team, or appropriate church leaders. In the context of this first stage there should also be repentance and submission, both of which are prerequisites for restoration.

The person or persons to whom admission or confession is made should be "spiritual" as indicated in Galatians 6:1; that is, they should be mature, proven, and well-regarded and respected by the church. This private aspect of the process reveals much about the person who has fallen: his or her humility, honesty, and desire to be helped.

There is a public aspect to the restoration process.

When the person who has fallen is a leader, there will come a time when the congregation or organization should be informed. This is never easy and is always painful, both for the fallen leader and for his or her family. This person's family ought to be considered, cared for, and protected during the process.

The public component of restoration can include a couple of things:

- A statement of the situation. In this statement there is no need for graphic or explicit terms or explanations, but there must be honesty and a level of transparency.
- In this public phase of the process there should also be the sharing of the future stages of the process along with a statement concerning the leader's ministerial activity.

There is a professional aspect to the restoration process.

The church today is becoming more open to including and inviting professional persons into the restoration process. The fallen leader is often required to meet with a professional counselor who will report back to an appointed member of the restoration team.

The spouse and children of the fallen leader should also be encouraged to take part in counseling. Where possible, the congregation should be willing to absorb or help with the cost of the counseling if insurance does not cover it. Once the process has been followed and fully engaged in by the leader, a means of reaffirmation can be discussed and decided upon.

This entire process should be a positive time of displaying that the church is serious about restoring the one who has fallen.

In the Winter 2006 issue of *Christianity Today* magazine, Eric Reed brings up several questions that must be addressed by the restoration process, including:

- Which offenses require absence from ministry?
- Is exposure to pornography an equally serious offense as an actual sexual affair?
- How long is the pastor to be out of ministry?
- What are the requirements for counseling and who will oversee it?
- Will there be any financial support for the pastor and family?
- Will the pastor's spouse be included in counseling and in meetings with the denomination or restoration team?
- After the restoration process, how will the pastor find a new position?

Reed's questions certainly provoke and prompt those who must deal with fallen and failed ministers to think and act with compassion, mercy, and understanding. The primary goal to keep in mind is to restore an erring brother or sister to right relationship with God, the church, his or her family, and the broader community.

Here are some final thoughts and elaborations for leaders, counselors, and select committees to consider in the restoration process:

1. Does the offense require an absence from ministry?

Few would argue that some sins appear to be more egregious than others. For instance, sexual sins such as adultery, homosexuality, and fornication are judged much more harshly than lying, dereliction of duty, and misappropriation of money. The question with which we are dealing is this: What is the nature of the offense that disqualifies a person from continuing in ministry?

2. Why do we have such a difficult time forgiving those in clerical leadership, but can easily forgive the church member who commits the most heinous type of sin?

I have known church members who were spouse abusers, adulterers, fornicators, thieves, and the list goes on. However, when such persons repent and seek forgiveness, we welcome them (at least a majority do so) with outstretched arms. Why is there a double standard when it comes to forgiveness and restoration for pastors? Have we, as Christians, given serious thought to the kinds of sins God forgave in the Bible examples that were previously cited and yet how hard we find it to forgive others? Are we greater and wiser than God, when it comes to forgiveness?

3. *What is considered to be a reasonable amount of time for a minister or pastor to remain inactive from serving in ministry?*

While it is difficult to put a timetable on the question of service, I would encourage ministers and pastors to be open to a cooling-off period. This can be a time to receive in-depth counseling, restoring relationships with those who have been wounded or betrayed. In many of our congregations when there has been a moral failure with the pastor or minister, his or her salary is cut almost immediately. Sometimes the pastor is given one month of salary and if the congregation is gracious, he or she may be granted a three-month salary. Church leaders should not request that the pastoral family give up their parsonage housing before the pastor and family can properly adjust to the abrupt changes they must undergo. When dealing with a minister and his or her family, congregations must not seek to administer punishment but instead couple understanding with love. Allow the minister an opportunity to gain some financial stability before cutting him or her off completely.

Conclusion

I realize that this brief chapter and its suggestions may generate more questions than answers. There may be some individuals who will disagree with selected parts, or all of it. At the same time, allow me to say that this is not an exhaustive or definitive document. It is simply an attempt to say that there is a way to deal with pastors who fall and fail, other than dismissing, destroying, denying, or permanently dismantling their right to be restored.

We must develop and employ a theology of grace, along with a theology of holiness. I, for one, believe that the two can coexist and serve a greater good without denying or negating each other.

About the Author

Bishop Timothy J. Clarke is senior pastor of First Church of God in Columbus, Ohio. He also leads the Berean Fellowship of Churches and serves the church-at-large as an evangelist and teacher.

Bishop Clarke received a Master of Ministry degree from the Southern California School of Ministry in Los Angeles, California, and was consecrated to the office of bishop in 2001. He has been awarded honorary doctorates from Mid-America Christian University, the Southern California School of Ministry, and Wilberforce University, and has been inducted to the Morehouse College Board of Preachers. After his ordination by the Church of God in 1977, Clarke began a long career of association with the National Association of the Church of God, West Middlesex, Pennsylvania. His service has included president of the National Inspirational Youth Convention; chairman and vice-chairman of the General Assembly; and president, vice-president, and presiding elder of the National Association of the Church of God.

Timothy Clarke and his wife, Clytemnestra, are the parents of two adult children and the proud grandparents of two grandchildren.

21. COVID-19 and Other Crises

by W. G. Robinson-McNeese, James L. Phillips, and Saundra L. McNeese

A dramatic challenge to ministry within the Church of God and other church groups emerged at the beginning of calendar year 2020, impacting how church will be conducted well into the future. The spread of the Coronavirus pandemic (a global disease) to the United States of America hit all aspects of the nation's existence, leading to widespread lifestyle adjustments. Faith communities were not spared any of these new disruptions.

The COVID-19 Pandemic

The pathogen (microorganism causing a disease) responsible for COVID-19, described as a novel virus because it had not been seen in this form before, was a member of the Coronavirus family (*corona* meaning "crown" in Latin; the virus was so named because of the microscopic shape of the virus capsule). This family of viruses is known to cause respiratory disease. The virus was often referred to as COVID-19, with the *CO* in the name standing for "Corona," the *VI* standing for "virus," the *D* standing for disease, and the number 19 representing the year the virus was first isolated in a patient (December 2019).

Virologists, epidemiologists, and others in the science and healthcare community generally agreed that the COVID-19 infections started in China, but early in the pandemic, origins of the pathogen had not been absolutely delineated. Speculation about the beginning of the virus included everything from it being a bioweapon released unintentionally to a case of "zoonotic spillover" (a virus started in an animal that somehow infects a human). Because science experts found no definitive evidence that COVID-19 was human-made, most origin theories hung on zoonotic spillover. Many believed the virology laboratory study of Coronaviruses increased the likelihood of the accidental spread of such diseases while simultaneously augmenting their lethality. Whatever its beginnings, the virus proved to be potentially deadly and easily transmitted.

COVID-19 infected large segments of the U.S. population, with marginalized groups suffering the most cases because of health disparities that negatively impacted their well-being long before the pandemic started. These social determinants of health included such things as poor education, food insecurity, substandard housing, inadequate transportation, lack of or inadequate health insurance, and culturally insensitive health care providers. Such inequities made these vulnerable members of our society easy targets for a virus out of control.

COVID-19 symptoms included fever, tiredness, cough, aches, pains, runny nose, nasal congestion, sore throat, chills, headache, and diarrhea. Symptoms could be mild or severe, or a patient could even be asymptomatic. Individuals at high risk for the infection included the immunocompromised (those having an impaired immune system), the elderly, and those with co-morbid conditions such as coronary artery disease, hypertension, diabetes, and lung diseases. Such accompanying diseases increased the possibility of an individual contracting the viral infection and made it less likely they would be able to fight the disease successfully.

COVID-19 was highly contagious and spread basically by respiratory droplets through coughing, sneezing, and close breathing—usually person-to-person contact. Individuals were most contagious when showing symptoms of the disease. Persons could also become infected by contact with surfaces contaminated with the virus. It was uncertain how long the coronavirus could remain alive on surfaces, but theories ranged from hours to days, depending on the type of surface. The incubation period (the time from contact with the virus until an individual showed symptoms) for COVID-19 was approximately two weeks.

In January 2020, the World Health Organization declared the coronavirus pandemic a "health emergency of international concern." That same month the COVID-19 pandemic reached the United States when a patient was diagnosed in Washington state. A U.S. White House task force formally recognized the virus threat later that same month and the nation's leaders suspended entry to the country for foreign nationals who had recently traveled to China. Other restrictions to public gatherings soon followed. Even so, the outbreak spread through the U.S. steadily and exponentially, leading to emergency declarations at national, state, and local levels. In the first full quarter of 2020, COVID-19 showed its pervasive, pandemic character to all segments of the nation's population, and millions of the country's citizens were predicted to die before the pandemic could be controlled.

Illnesses such as the common cold can result from some Coronaviruses, but more serious symptoms occurred as a result of infection with COVID-19. Most people recovered from infection with this pathogen, but a significant number died from the disease. Due to lack of familiarity with COVID-19 (its novel character), there was no available vaccine at first. Laboratories worldwide worked feverishly to develop not only vaccines but also drugs to treat infected patients.

Seriously ill COVID-19 patients required hospitalization, usually after presenting with pulmonary problems, sometimes requiring intubation.

In the midst of any pandemic, prophylactic (intended to prevent disease) care is required. Physical distancing is the main feature of such prevention efforts, combined with hand washing, use of facemasks, covering one's nose and mouth when coughing or sneezing, and abandonment of handshaking. Minimizing contact with one's face, eyes, and nose is a high-priority technique as well to reduce spread of such a disease. Disinfecting furniture, desks, car interiors, and other surfaces was also a very important practice. These proven strategies were meant to accompany a "shelter in place" philosophy that was thought to blunt the spread of the virus by reducing human interactions. This temporary strategy was carried out in varying degrees by different communities with shifting success.

The Impact on Churches

Retail stores, churches, theaters, parks, and malls were among places citizens were called upon to either not attend, or to maintain at least a six-foot distance from one another when going to them. Because the COVID-19 calamity led to sheltering-at-home strategies, churches temporarily closed, modified, or cancelled services. Pastors and other church leaders were called upon to act quickly and creatively to protect their members, but also to schedule alternative worship services and church meetings. Online gatherings utilizing modalities such as Facebook and Zoom and parking-lot meetings in cars are examples of services that sprang up and began to flourish despite the pandemic's conditions.

Sadly, many church groups in communities classified as low income, disadvantaged, and/or immigrant found their members being hit harder than others because of woefully inadequate or absent health care. Already victimized by disparities, individuals in these communities, especially African Americans, Latinos, Native Americans, and Alaskan Natives, were at much greater risk of infection by COVID-19. These groups experienced higher complication rates as well, and the church was a leader among many servant-minded groups that stepped up to help.

While dealing with the physical rigors of the Coronavirus, Christians simultaneously had their faith shaken and their bodies weakened in the wake of this outbreak. As we worked with our various pastors and congregational leaders, we found that the COVID-19 pandemic challenged theological and doctrinal beliefs about how God would care for his people and see them through calamities. Christians throughout the United States began to pray in earnest, citing 2 Chronicles 7:14 (NIV): "If my people, who are called by my name, will humble themselves and pray and seek my face and turn from their wicked ways, then I will hear from heaven, and I will forgive their sin and will heal their land."

Many wondered why their prayers were not being answered with direct healing or total elimination of the viral pandemic, and why church leaders and laypersons alike were dying in spite of their fervent entreaties. Some were temporarily stunned into inactivity. Some tried to carry on worship practices as if nothing significant had happened. However, the steady spread of the pandemic led many to decide that God was not going to immediately stem the pandemic, but instead was calling them to faithfully go through the ups and downs of the virus spread. Even though no divine protection would shield them from all the virus's effects, they determined to trust and believe in God, but also to follow best medical practices while looking after themselves and their parishioners.

The Response of Churches

Not able to physically worship together because of restrictions placed on them by government authorities, many Christians turned to another part of God's Word, James 2:18–20 (NIV): "Someone will say, 'You have faith; I have deeds.' Show me your faith without deeds, and I will show you my faith by my deeds. You believe that there is one God. Good! Even the demons believe that—and shudder. You foolish person, do you want evidence that faith without deeds is useless?"

We found that members of the clergy began to balance the desire to continue traditional forms of church worship against the need to be wise, safe, and good role models. These leaders earnestly looked for ways to continue to win souls in a world landscape that had been drastically changed by an ever-expanding viral disease.

Pastors learned quickly how to not only incorporate technology into their worship services, but also how to use technology as the main way to conduct the services. Some began to formulate worship services, Bible studies, and Sunday schools that were interactive, congregational experiences done via the Internet. Many began conference calling and tasked small groups to make sure all church members were informed about and felt included in the worship experience. We watched and studied the various church services that were now available for all to see.

Zoom, Skype, and similar platforms were immediately launched from church websites, offices, and personal laptop computers. How exciting to find that even smaller congregations broadcast their services via YouTube, with many of the videos becoming overnight sensations. Facebook Live and the Marco Polo app also were used to reach parishioners and thus many small, street-corner churches developed a presence on the World Wide Web.

Faith leaders distinguished themselves in other areas as well. Because countless businesses had been closed due to stay-at-home orders, many congregants lost their jobs or worked abbreviated hours. Responding to dire straits facing members, churches became resource centers for their respective communities. Church office workers and other employees began to channel information from city, state, and national pandemic leaders to local neighborhoods to keep them informed of the status of the pandemic and to explain where citizens could go for help.

Congregations turned their parking lots into food distribution sites to serve local families in need and opened their doors to become testing sites for COVID-19. Many church members who were doctors or nurses stepped up to help in retirement communities or wherever needed. In many instances around the country, the church led the way in caring for seniors—making phone calls, organizing regular contact days, running errands, delivering meals, and cleaning homes.

Once church leaders made it through the initial period of shock, they began to work steadily to find solutions. We learned innovative ways to conduct physical distancing that were easily applied at church functions, and PPE (personal protective equipment) became the new norm for official gatherings outside the home. Some congregations even began to produce masks in their local sewing circles. The fabric patterns and mask formats ran from comical to biblical in nature, and some of the masks employed special filters that aided breathing for the elderly and those short of breath.

Congregation leaders soon learned that parishioners unable to work because of restrictions would also be less likely to tithe, but determined to move forward with their ministries, trusting God to provide needed resources. Even though many churches experienced a drop in contributions because no regular church services also meant no regular offering collections, these organizations continued to address the needs of their members and surrounding communities. This was done all while offering spiritual, emotional, financial, and other types counseling for the saints.

Congregations created databases of resources made available to the public at little or no cost:

- Daycare services for essential employees who had to work
- Non-contact activities for teens (e.g., online interactive sports)
- Tutorial support for students grades kindergarten through college
- Day-labor assistance as it became available
- Literature regarding other available assistance to get through the pandemic

Once church leaders accepted their new role as thought leaders and solution finders in the face of COVID-19, rather than victims, they began to flow in the spirit of creating a different worship and learning experience within their buildings. God had uniquely positioned them to do so.

Under a new, need-based revelation that took into consideration the health and safety of all who would gather, we worked with church leaders to come up with the following suggestions for future church meetings and initiatives that would protect and improve the health of all who attend:

- Greeters can take on the new responsibility of being definite doorkeepers who "regulate traffic," also periodically cleaning door handles and preventing them from being touched by everyone entering.

- Ushers can give special attention to physical distancing once people are inside the sanctuary, and during offering collection make sure everyone has an opportunity to give safely. This might be done through an "offering walk" or by ensuring that the collection plate is handled by as few people as possible before re-cleaning it.

- Choirs can try using the "flash mob" format, where each of them sing and praise the Lord from wherever they are in the sanctuary. What a blessing!

- Worship leaders can position themselves as usual while using adequate PPE as necessary.

- Congregants can be encouraged to sit as family units but to be considerate of other families and make sure there is plenty of "distancing room."

- As they stand behind the "sacred desk," pastors and ministers can proclaim what the Lord has given his people for such a time as this.

- In addition to in-person gatherings, many worship experiences can be continued online through "Zoom" or similar forums; some people who are noticeably quiet in physically open settings feel more comfortable to talk when interacting in this way.

- Teaching in youth groups can begin to emphasize the need for more young people to seek health-related careers. Churches can create and offer summer programs that are made available for students interested in medicine, nursing, and other related areas.

- Churches can be proactive in offering college scholarships for studies in all health fields for students from groups underrepresented in medicine.

This is not an exhaustive list of changes that can and should be considered as leaders plan the future of worship experiences in the church. Our leaders must still give thought to weighty subjects such as the possibility of modifying the performance of church ordinances. Biblically, we must continue to share Communion reverently while maintaining our physical distancing. This has been challenging to some, yet called out creativity in others.

In addition to local church decisions that include such lighter topics as refreshments and meeting and greeting, leaders must decide what national gatherings will look like going forward and even whether they will take place at all.

Conclusion

It is certain that church worship will forever be impacted by the onset of the Coronavirus pandemic in early 2020. Such crises, whether they concern health, safety, economics, or some other area, often cannot be predicted. They impact all people in many ways, and they impact the church in some unique and challenging ways.

COVID-19 taught us many important things, perhaps most importantly that God is still on the throne, and he will always lead us through. In times of crisis, our role is to listen and follow his principles in love with unfaltering faith.

About the Authors

Rev. W. G. Robinson-McNeese, MD, is a retired pastor and emergency physician currently leading True Love Ministries, an interfaith outreach in Springfield, Illinois. He also works part-time for Southern Illinois University, mentoring high school, undergraduate, and medical students. During the COVID-19 outbreak, McNeese gave special attention to community members and students from marginalized racial groups who suffered disproportionately from the impact of the disease.

James L. Phillips, MD, is professor emeritus and retired senior associate dean for diversity and community outreach at Baylor College of Medicine. At Baylor, he prioritized the recruitment of those underserved in medicine to become physicians. Phillips has been the physician for the National Association of the Church of God at its annual convention and served on the trustee boards at Bay Ridge Christian College, Mid-America Christian University, and Washington and Jefferson College.

Saundra L. McNeese, MBA, has been active in the Church of God as an ordained minister and pastoral care chaplain. As business specialist for the Texas Ministries of the Church of God, she works tirelessly with pastors and leaders throughout Texas and other states. Saundra's role as disaster team chair kept her busy throughout the COVID-19 pandemic assisting with support to local congregations.

Notes: